NO ONE TO TELL

NO
ONE

JANET MERLO

TO TELL

BREAKING MY SILENCE ON LIFE IN THE RCMP

BREAKWATER

1 Stamp's Lane, St. John's, NL, Canada, A1E 3C9
WWW.BREAKWATERBOOKS.COM

ISBN 978-1-55081-434-7
A CIP catalogue record for this book is available from Library and Archives Canada.

Canada Council for the Arts Conseil des Arts du Canada Canadä

We acknowledge the support of the Canada Council for the Arts, which last year invested $154 million to bring the arts to Canadians throughout the country. We acknowledge the Government of Canada through the Canada Book Fund and the Government of Newfoundland and Labrador through the Department of Tourism, Culture and Recreation for our publishing activities.

PRINTED AND BOUND IN CANADA.

MIX
Paper from responsible sources
FSC® C016245

I WOULD LIKE TO DEDICATE this book to the serving members of the RCMP who keep our communities safe. To my friends, who were my anchors through some of the worst years of my life. To my parents, who have stood by me throughout with unwavering support. To my ex-husband, who has also suffered so much through all of this. And to my former colleagues, brave women, who have also told their stories in the hope of creating worthwhile change.

Most of all, I want to dedicate this book to my beautiful daughters Ashley and Erin. I am so blessed to have you. You have been my reason for fighting, my reason for living, and my reason for working to get my life back on track. You are both amazing, beautiful young ladies. This is for you.

Contents

INTRODUCTION

THE LETTER FROM THE RCMP on Christmas Eve 1990 telling Janet Merlo she'd been accepted for membership caused a storm of conflicting feelings. She was thrilled—she'd known for a while she wanted to be a police officer. Now the door to a stable, rewarding future was swinging open. But she was suddenly full of self-doubt. Am I ready? What if I lack the mental and physical qualities, the integrity and confidence and dedication to meet the standards of the legendary police force? Am I good enough to be a Mountie?

The last thing on Janet Merlo's mind as she struggled with the sudden, now daunting, challenge was the peril of harassment and disrespect. Police officers are empowered to protect the vulnerable from bullies. Along with the right to wear the garb of law enforcement, they automatically become entitled to respect. How could she have anticipated that in such an institution as the RCMP she would find, among her colleagues, many—one in ten she reckons—who would be bullies? How could she have anticipated disrespect, vulgarity, emotional and often physical harassment in a workplace dedicated to the ideals of justice?

Eight months later, August 26, 1991, she was one of twenty-nine fresh-faced Mounties proudly marching through a graduation ceremony at the RCMP training depot in Regina, Saskatchewan, sworn and trained and irreversibly committed to "uphold the right." One of her troop mates was Catherine Galliford—a friend who, in the distant future, would become an ally. Like Merlo, Galliford would become another high-profile casualty in the quiet, grinding struggle by women to find viable careers within a culture traditionally defined by men to value exclusive, often primitive, notions of "manhood."

No One to Tell is a sad account of history and human nature, a story of idealism dying slowly, and of the anger and the cynicism that fill the gaps left behind by lost ideals, eventually infecting every aspect of an individual's existence. It is the story of many women in many walks of life, not just the Mounties, but it is of particular importance considering the deference and power that we concede to people we deem to be exceptional—teachers, legislators, clergy, and police, to name just a few.

It is also, as such stories often are, about institutional betrayal and the systemic failure of leadership—an all too human tendency in leaders to avoid confronting realities that, acknowledged, could undermine institutional authority. It is a syndrome that threatens the integrity of all institutions, the impulse to sacrifice a principled individual grievance to protect an institutional façade, an impulse with the frequent and paradoxical result that institutions are, themselves, thus corrupted and reduced.

The institution Janet Merlo went to work for in 1991 was a troubled place. The modern RCMP started out in 1873 as the Royal North West Mounted Police, a paramilitary organization that would grow to be the principal source of law and order in three territories and eight provinces. It would take 101 years to accept the possibility that women had a role in law enforcement.

There was widespread scepticism when the change came, in May 1974. There were jokes (I personally heard the references by Mountie acquaintances to "Dickless Tracy" and new avenues for "undercover work"). There were dark predictions of sexual tensions and inevitable trysts when men and women were assigned to work together—unsupervised, in cars, at night—and a sharp escalation in conflict in the domestic lives of married (male) Mounties. The underlying fear seemed to be that women are inherently unstable emotionally and sexually and would disturb the natural decorum and collegiality of the work place. In many cases, that's exactly what happened, but not because of inherent instability among the new female officers; it was instead because their arrival exposed a shocking immaturity and chauvinism among many of their male colleagues. One could speculate how such flaws in character affected how these officers interacted with members of the public. It is for now sufficient only to review how these basic human failings affected the work and the lives of the new female recruits—and the wider public perception of the RCMP as an institution.

Janet Merlo wasn't working long in her first job at the detachment in Nanaimo, BC, when she began hearing isolated references to alleged harassment of women officers who were inevitably "bitches" to be shunned and, when opportunities arose, to be punished for their distracting petty grievances. She understood instinctively the code by which conformity and collegiality are vital to the bonding that creates a comfort zone when times get tough. Knowing that a colleague "has your back" is essential to the confident performance of duties that are often dangerous. Even when her own legitimate complaint (about manpower shortages) was dismissed by a superior with the comment "Boys, Merlo is on the rag again…" an instinct for self- preservation shut her down.

Even in the best of circumstances, police work is, by

definition, stressful. Nobody ever calls a cop to report that they're having a great day. It would take about ten years before the accumulated wear and tear of working in a job that see-sawed erratically from dangerous to tedious with people among whom many seemed incapable of professional respect for women, became a persistent day-to-day malaise. She knew that she was "a fucking woman with a big mouth" and had been explicitly told her superiors were hoping that she'd quit the force. Things were going downhill at home. It would take many more years before she'd realize that she was not alone.

All through the nineties, women had persevered, isolated by a feeling that their problems were individual, mostly caused by personality conflicts. Few dared to consider that the circumstances that made the workplace stressful had roots that were both historical and systemic—and that many, many women in the RCMP had similar and worse complaints. It's unclear how many knew that between 1999 and 2003 the behaviour of one officer, Robert Blundel, had led to complaints by at least four women of harassment and abuse including rape. After years of investigation and inquiry, their complaints were largely substantiated. The rape allegation was watered down to "inappropriate" sexual relations on the job. The consequences for the accused officer were arguably trivial. For the women who complained, lives and careers went downhill swiftly.

One observation, in a review of the proceedings involving Blundel, by Chief Superintendent Ian Atkins in 2003, is worth quoting in full:

> From facts of the four specific complaints investigated and some of the other incidents not yet investigated, it appears there may be some reluctance by some female members and employees to make complaints of sexual harassment. The psychological reasons for this are beyond the scope of this Review, however a lay

> assessment may be that the complainants believe they weren't given the appropriate opportunity to make a complaint, or that they may have had reason to believe that their complaint would not be believed; or that they may have believed no substantive action would have been taken to change the situation. Each of the complainants and several other interviewees referred to 'the old boys' culture of the RCMP as being very difficult to penetrate, and perhaps being one of the sources of the beliefs enumerated above.

Remember, this observation was about women who complained of sexual harassment that in some cases crossed the line to justify credible allegations of sexual assault. Women officers with grievances that included criminal behaviour by their colleagues were afraid to rock the boat. What then of the legions of women who simply felt unwelcome and degraded and unable to do their jobs effectively? They all seemed unaware that the RCMP even had a policy that stated "harassment on any grounds is offensive, degrading and threatening and will not be tolerated...." The definition of harassment was broad and included "...leering, degrading remarks, jokes or taunting, insulting gestures, displays of offensive pictures or materials, and unwelcome enquiries or comments about someone's personal life."

Women whose workplace experiences precisely fit that definition were, it seems, deterred from taking action by a paralyzing belief that no one cared and no one would believe them.

The RCMP regulations are consistent with the Canadian Human Rights Act. The federal Treasury Board Policy on the Prevention and Resolution of Harassment in the Workplace goes further than both. In its preamble it includes, in its definition of harassment, "...rude, degrading or offensive remarks or emails, threats or intimidation."

It continues: "Harassment in the workplace is unacceptable

and will not be tolerated. All persons working for the Public Service, whether or not they are employees, should enjoy a harassment-free workplace."

Notwithstanding all the pieties, Janet Merlo, like the others, suffered for the most part silently, her disillusionment metastasizing to corrosive bitterness. She will point out in her story that the majority of the men she worked with were kind, considerate, and supportive. But the minority were sufficiently influential to set the tone for many working days and nights. In Nanaimo, the minority included some of her superiors.

In 2007 there appeared to be a sunburst of hopefulness. For the first time in its history, the RCMP would be led by a commissioner selected from outside its ranks. The appointment of William Elliott, a civilian, signalled a commitment to fundamental change in an organization that seemed to have become a magnet for controversy. Merlo, as she writes in these pages, was looking for "a new style of leadership":

> After all, I knew first-hand the effects of the old system. I had suffered bullying, harassment, and the callous disregard of management. I had seen preferential treatment supplant fairness, and I had endured a staggering lack of compassion that destroyed my mental health and almost tore my family apart...I was finally desperate enough to blurt out everything and beg for help.

She wrote a long letter to the new commissioner and bluntly told her story, starting with the high hopes that drew her to the force, and building to the slow erosion of her confidence, her mental and emotional fitness for the law enforcement duties she had sworn to carry out. She expressed enthusiastic hope that the new commissioner's appointment marked a new beginning for the institution.

She sent the letter by express post directly to William Elliott. The response, when it came more than a month later, was a form letter from the minister of public safety, Stockwell Day. She never did hear back from Elliott.

It would be late 2011 before she dared to hope again, and this time the inspiration came not from her superiors but from another woman, an old friend and classmate from back in 1991—Catherine Galliford.

Cpl. Galliford, who had become a high-profile public spokesperson for the RCMP, had filed an internal complaint that she had faced constant sexual advances from several senior officers from the moment she graduated from the RCMP Academy in 1991. In November 2011, on a CBC news broadcast, she would make an observation that would resonate for many women in the force: "If I had a dime for every time one of my bosses asked me to sit on his knee, I'd be on a yacht in the Bahamas right now."

Her public declaration was shocking, but it would release a flood of testimony from women who had been, for decades, publicly silent, including two of the women who had, years earlier, struggled internally to advance serious complaints of sexual abuse by Staff Sgt. Robert Blundel, who had been a constable at the time of his "discreditable conduct."

In March 2012, Janet Merlo, who by then had left the force, filed a class-action lawsuit in the BC courts expecting dozens of women to come forward with supporting stories of their unhappy experience as officers in Canada's national police force. Within months, there were hundreds, women who were fed up with silence about the sexism and abuse that had derailed their careers. They have since joined the lawsuit that started its journey through the courts in June 2013.

Shortly after he became commissioner, late in 2011, Bob Paulson was unequivocal in his condemnation of sexual harassment. He has introduced new standards and procedures and training protocols to confront a problem that had forty years to establish deep roots in the culture and memory of the force. But in June 2013, before a Senate committee in Ottawa, his good intentions seemed to have, to some degree, degenerated to exasperation.

"Let's face it," he said. "Some people's ambitions exceed their abilities. I cannot lead a force that accommodates and seeks to compensate people for those unachieved ambitions. Policing is a very tough job. It is very rewarding but also very demanding. Frankly, it is not for everyone."

Commissioner Paulson takes sexual harassment and assault quite seriously, as he should. But in what seems to be a dismissive attitude toward bullying, he misses an important point. Bullying, anywhere, is always a problem, but when it is related to race or gender or beliefs, it is a hate crime waiting for a time and place to happen.

Janet Merlo's story is about bullying and the banality of a toxic work environment that includes real-time misery, tragedy, and violence—a combination that can and often does prove lethal to health, character, and hope for any officer, male or female. Add to this harassment rooted in deep, primitive sexism and the burden can become unbearable for people who in many cases, ironically, have exactly the personalities and the character and motivation to be among the very best police officers.

Janet Merlo named the story of her personal struggle *No One to Tell*, but after decades of silence, she and other women may now have finally found a voice and, more important, a sympathetic audience—the public that they served, the ultimate source of judgment, power, and change.

Linden MacIntyre
June 2013

Prologue

When I went public with allegations about harassment in the RCMP, what shocked me most were the comments on Internet news sites. I had put myself out there, described to the media some of the worst things that had ever happened to me—things that were deeply personal and remained profoundly embarrassing—and I had allowed my name and my face to be known.

It was so hard to do. In 1991, I'd joined one of the most amazing organizations in the world. When the iconic Royal Canadian Mounted Police chose me to serve on its force, I leapt at the chance. More than two decades later, I still carry that pride though it's buried beneath years of disappointment. The organization I'd been so honoured to join did not feel the same pride in the women it employed—though for too many years, I'd thought it was just me. Then I discovered there were many others, and I went from being alone to being part of a group of sad, stressed women who felt they had no real power to change their circumstances. Some made the decision to quit, to walk away. The rest of us resigned ourselves to the reality that if we wanted to keep the jobs we'd grown to love, we would have to do so in silence.

Eventually, the cost of keeping quiet was just too high. But when I finally did file an internal complaint, my concerns were dismissed as "unsubstantiated," and my voice fell silent again until 2011 when a troop mate of mine, Catherine Galliford, made her story public. Her courage inspired over one hundred and fifty more women to find the strength to tell their stories. I was one of them.

In the preceding years, I'd lost both the career I loved and my marriage, faced significant medical issues, and buried loved ones. I was suffering from post-traumatic stress disorder. I was wrung out, angry, and exhausted, but I knew I had to muster the courage. I steeled myself for attacks from some elements of the organization whose integrity I was calling into question, but I was completely unprepared for the anonymous attacks online.

The commenters let loose with a fury of accusations, disparaging me and the other women who had come forward to share our stories. The caustic remarks didn't just question the validity of what we'd said, they maligned our character, questioned our motives, labelled us as weak complainers jumping on a bandwagon. Some went so far as to denigrate my appearance (I was, after all, too ugly to be sexually harassed). It was crushing. I had put myself—my whole identity—out there in the public realm, and these people were hiding behind their computers and the smokescreen of their usernames, spewing scorn.

When I mentioned to a reporter how upset I was about the posted comments, she gave me an invaluable weapon. She told me to remember that a lot of comments were probably made by fellows who live in their parents' basements, losers who sit around all day in their underwear typing nasty things into their computers because they have nothing else to contribute. I have held on to that mental image. It has helped, though I have no idea how accurate it really is or if those scornful opinions are shared by the people I walk past in the grocery store.

In the years since my story first emerged, while I contemplated and then wrote this memoir, I read all the accounts. I read Linda Duxbury's 2007 independent report concerning workplace issues at the RCMP, the organization's own November 2012 Gender-Based Assessment, and the February 2013 Human Rights Watch report that found grave disregard on the force for the safety of aboriginal females. I followed all the news coverage of allegations about harassment and bullying within the RCMP, and I have continued to read every comment posted after those news stories. I have noticed that, as more accounts emerged, negative comments became fewer. The scathing disbelief diminished. This gives me some hope that change is possible.

Change is the reason I have spoken out to the media, launched a lawsuit, and written this memoir. My goal—a goal shared by my former colleagues who have also spoken out—is to make life better for women in the RCMP and in other police forces in Canada, for both established officers and young recruits. And for other young women, too—young women like my daughters.

It is important to note that the allegations in this book are included in the legal statement of claim I have filed but are, as yet, unproven in court. They are my truthful recollections of incidents that occurred—aided by the notebooks I kept throughout my career—though names have been omitted and some details smudged to obscure identities for legal reasons.

The purpose of my book is certainly not to bash the RCMP. I am still very proud of the organization, its place in Canadian history, and the amazing members I worked with over the years.

The vast majority of members I've known are decent, hardworking police officers. But a small percentage—ten percent or so, in my experience—use sexual harassment, bullying, and intimidation to make life unbearable for many good members and for women, especially. It's a small minority; unfortunately, it's also a potent one. Bullying and harassment in the force take an astounding toll on the lives of both women *and* men and, I would argue, on the ability of Canada's national police force to serve and protect our communities effectively.

I have to be stronger than those who hide behind their false screens and try to break others by hurling abuse. It's well past time to speak out for change.

Exiting and Beginning

1

I RAN INTO THE SERGEANT near the back door of the detachment office, so I asked him if he wanted in that week. For years, I'd been collecting the money for the lottery pool. I took two dollars from anyone who wanted to play, and I bought the tickets. Why not? We could all use a few million extra.

The sergeant dug out a five-dollar bill and handed it to me, watching intently through his pale, always watery eyes as I folded it and tucked it into my right breast pocket. The shift was just beginning, so I hadn't yet slipped into my bulletproof vest. I told him I wasn't sure if I had his change just then in my pants.

Stupid, giving this guy an opening like that. He never really needed much of an opening—any conversation was an excuse for a come on, for some salacious remark.

He cupped a meaty hand and held it close to my breast, not touching but moving it as if rubbing the spot where his money had just disappeared. "You wouldn't have to give me any change if you'd let me put that in your pocket."

Repulsed, I avoided his eyes, focusing instead on how the

overhead lights gleamed off the pasty expanse of his forehead. I could feel the outrage rising in me, the profanity bubbling on my tongue, but I swallowed it down. I'd gotten good at that. After all, he'd been my direct supervisor for quite a while, and he had the power to grant or refuse whatever I asked for—days off, training courses, a lunch hour that coincided with a school concert. I fished around in my pants, searching in vain for the three dollars I owed him so we could end this conversation. I told him I'd have to get it to him later and started to leave, but he wasn't done. He stepped in and blocked my exit, dropped his hand, and made a gesture like his fingers were about to dive into my pants pocket. "Like I said, you wouldn't have to give me change...."

I knew I'd spend the next hour formulating comebacks, thinking of all the things I could have said while the sergeant loomed over me with that expectant, juvenile grin on his face. But that was a futile pursuit—I would never get to utter any of them out loud. He held my entire career in the fleshy palm of that hand, so I clamped my mouth shut, again, and I ducked around him. But I know my face registered my disgust.

Not long after that, the sergeant trashed me in my annual performance assessment. It's the only negative assessment I ever received in my nearly two decades with the RCMP. He claimed I wasn't ambitious enough. His proof—that I had failed to write a personal choice test that might allow me to rise up in the ranks. And then he took away my role as acting corporal when the corporal on our watch was away. I'd been performing this duty off and on for years, but though I had the experience, the sergeant decided I no longer qualified for the role, and he gave it to a younger male member who he said showed more interest in pursuing a promotion.

Years later, after my career with the RCMP came to a crashing end, I let loose on the anonymous Exit Interview questionnaire that asked me to reflect on my service:

> The RCMP is 100 years behind in its treatment of women. Sexual harassment is rampant. There is no accountability other than to quietly transfer the offending members and return results of investigations to those who speak out as "unfounded." I am example of such treatment. Witnesses and other females who experienced similar behavior are afraid to speak out for fear of punishment. It continues to be a dirty little secret.

Those words are written in my hand in response to question 12: "What are some negative aspects of your service with the RCMP, if any?"

I didn't mince words. My three-page questionnaire, once completed, was nine pages long, the handwriting dense and cramped. The form had come with my retirement package, and I filled it out in March 2010—my lowest, most frustrated, most broken point. I knew if I didn't send it right away, I would calm down and want to change some of the answers so they weren't so harsh and honest. Instead, I shoved it in an envelope and mailed it off without even making a copy. Later, I wished I had one.

After I launched a lawsuit against the RCMP, I wrote to the officer in charge of the National Staffing Policy Branch in Ottawa, requesting a copy of my exit interview. I didn't expect to hear back. I thought maybe they had shredded it. To my surprise, I got a call a few weeks later from a very pleasant man who said he'd love to provide a copy, but the forms are filed anonymously. He was flipping through those that had come in around the time of my retirement, and he wondered: was there anything about mine that would make it stand out? I said yes, it's nine pages long, hand written, and I was pissed off.

He found it right away and told me he'd even flagged it when he got it, sent off a couple of memos about my responses.

He didn't tell me who got those memos or what, if anything, was done about them.

He asked why I wanted it. I guess he hadn't recognized my name, which was all over the news then. I just said it had been a very stressful time and I was dealing with a lot of healing, and that I couldn't quite remember what I'd said. Good enough—he scanned the whole thing and emailed it to me. And there it was, the fiery document with all my issues laid out. I'd detailed the same concerns in a letter to the RCMP commissioner in which I'd first mentioned sexual harassment in 2007. Yet despite the effort I'd made to alert senior people to the problems I'd encountered, no one that I knew of had taken any action at all.

Not all of my responses on that questionnaire were fiery, so maybe I've started in the wrong place.

Question 11 asked: "What are some positive aspects of your service with the RCMP?" I wrote,

> I would have to say the most positive aspect of my service was meeting the thousands of people I encountered, hearing their stories, and learning from them.... I feel I am much wiser, far more compassionate and understanding.

It's true that if I had never joined the RCMP, I would have missed out on so much that I value in my life. Despite everything, I would do it all again, absolutely.

I WAS BORN IN CARBONEAR, a small commercial center in eastern Newfoundland where my mother, Catherine Keough, had grown up. In its long history, Carbonear survived numerous attacks. In1697 and again in 1705, most of its structures were burned to the ground by the French. It rose each time from the ashes and began again. My grandfather, Leonard Keough, worked for the Canadian National Railway in Carbonear and operated the transatlantic telegraph communication from his little office in a historic downtown building. He died when I was still an infant, but my grandmother would often point out the window where his office had been.

My mother met my father, Ben Farrell, after finishing high school. They married and settled in my father's nearby hometown of Harbour Grace, where they built their home just a stone's throw from Dad's parents and raised three children.

Harbour Grace is equally steeped in history. It first appeared as a permanent settlement in 1583 and in 1610 was the settlement of the famous pirate Peter Easton. Later, it boasted an airstrip that saw such visitors as Amelia Earhart. Unlike the mercantile center of Carbonear, Harbour Grace was built on fishing and fish processing, but both towns operated on the values of hard work and strong faith. Despite its name, Harbour Grace has known its share of difficult times, including the loss of many men to the cold Atlantic Ocean and the collapse of the fishery and its way of life.

Religious conflict was an intense part of these histories, too. Communities were physically divided, with the Catholics building in one part of town and the Anglicans, Protestants, and others building separately. Each church ran its own school in what was known as a denominational school system—a system that remained in place after Newfoundland joined Canada in 1949. Change was slow to come. In fact it wasn't until the 1998-1999 school year that the province of Newfoundland undertook education in a uniform, publicly funded, non-denominational system.

I recently saw a picture of a sweatshirt being sold online. It said, "You can't scare me, I was taught by nuns." I knew just what it meant. My brothers and I, like our parents before us, had all attended Catholic schools where the Presentation Sisters enforced silence and strict discipline. They were often the teachers and always the school principals, and we learned very early not to speak up or question a command. We learned to keep our heads down and be silent. As long as you were good and quiet, as I was, you could stay out of trouble.

My parents, however, weren't strict. They were firm and had high expectations of us, but they were very respectful of their children. I was the middle child, the only girl, and I would have done anything to avoid disappointing them. I placed high expectations on myself. I never wanted to let my parents, or anyone else, down. I wanted to succeed in whatever I did. Maybe it was just my personality, or maybe it was a kind of thank you to them for all they had done for me. Either way, that tendency set the stage for what I would put up with in my adult life.

Nonetheless, I had a wonderful time growing up. We worked hard in school all week long, and on the weekends, my parents would load up the trailer, and we would head to a different provincial park. In the summers, we would go camping with a group of other families or spend our days riding our bikes, playing horseshoes, swimming, or exploring the trails in the parks. Our winters were spent on snowmobiles or in the woods, huddled around a fire on which we would boil water in an old kettle or an old apple juice can. Sometimes we cut a hole in the ice to catch fish, but it was drinking hot chocolate on cold days, our cheeks rosy above our snowsuits, that really stands out in my mind. We lived our lives outdoors, and I developed my lifelong love of camping and kayaking that continues to this day.

MY FIRST FLASHBULB MEMORY—THE kind of memory that remains bright and stark in your mind because it attaches to some big emotion—is from February 1982, when a vicious storm hit Newfoundland.

Off the island's coast, 166 miles east of St. John's, a massive oil rig called the *Ocean Ranger*, built to withstand the harsh North Atlantic, was drilling an exploration well on the Grand Banks. The crew of eighty-four included many men from my hometown. One of the men on board was a very good friend of my father. It was his first trip out to work on the rigs.

Just after midnight on February 15, a mayday call came from the *Ocean Ranger*. A large wave had broken through. A short time later, the last transmission announced that the crew were heading to the life boats.

Schools closed because of the weather, and in the morning, I remember kneeling on the couch with my mother. We faced the back of the couch, warming our hands on the heated air rising from the electric baseboard as we watched the storm carry on outside. Behind us, the television was on so we could catch news. We knew the rig was gone, that it had listed and sunk in a raging cold sea, but we wanted news of the surviving men who had abandoned it. We especially wanted news of my father's friend.

When the news came, it was devastating: all eighty-four crew lost. No community in Newfoundland was unaffected. Families everywhere lost fathers, brothers, and sons—all men who had jumped at their chance to work offshore and bring home a decent wage after the floundering years of the fishery.

I was fourteen years old and overwhelmed by the sense of loss, by the idea my father's dear friend would never come home. None of the men who worked on that rig, trying to earn a better life for themselves and their families, were coming home. Instead, the Valentine's Day cards their kids had made for them at school now adorned altars at memorial services.

Suddenly, I was profoundly aware that any path a person chose could lead to danger, to disaster, and that you could never be sure of coming back okay. A person could get hurt anywhere, I decided right then, so it was important to put a lot of thought into what to do, what path I should take toward the future—and that, whatever I chose to do, it better matter because there might not be a chance to change my mind.

I graduated from high school and enrolled in Memorial University of Newfoundland in 1985. I still had no clear vision of what, exactly, I wanted to do, but I knew I wanted to do something that would be challenging for a lifetime.

I'd always had a keen interest in corrections and criminal behavior. Throughout my youth, I'd vocally favoured a "hang 'em" approach. I even recall, in grade nine, engaging in an ongoing debate with one of my teachers about capital punishment, about how I would happily take the job of flicking the switch on the electric chair. I suppose I was still in the black-and-white, good-and-bad stage of development (a stage many people, I later learned, never outgrow). The law is the law, I believed; if you broke it, you had to pay, and the price should be high. My opinion was strong and uninformed, and it started to shift as soon as I started to gather new information.

I studied sociology and learned how poverty and desperation warp the choices people make. I learned that, sometimes, mental health issues distort a person's sense of right and wrong. I was introduced to the idea that most of us are not simply good or bad, but are products of our environments, that we learn early how to feel sympathy, empathy, responsibility—and then we carry that ability, or the lack of it, into adulthood. I began to see grey areas, to understand complex social issues—drug abuse, child abuse, the cycle of poverty—and I began to wonder if perhaps a lot of crime could be prevented if only resources were focused on the causes rather than reacting to the aftermath. And I developed a keen interest in the nature versus nurture debate, an interest that has never waned.

I've done a lot of self-reflection in recent years, but I have yet to decide whether I'm more nature or nurture. Now in the latter half of my forties, I still look in the mirror at times and wonder which force led my life down the path it took, and whether I could have done anything differently, changed any of it.

It was sheer accident—or maybe serendipity—that led me to the RCMP.

As I finished up my degree in sociology with a certificate in criminology, I struggled to find an appropriate job. It's never easy in your early twenties, when your ambitions so far outstrip your experience.

One day a friend asked me to come along while she wrote the entrance exam for the RCMP. She was nervous and wanted the company. I wasn't keen to go, but I figured it might be at least a little interesting to witness the process. We drove down to Pleasantville in the east end of St. John's where there's a scattering of military buildings, and we found the RCMP headquarters. The man who administered the test asked if I wanted to write it, too. I shook my head—absolutely not—explained to him I was only there for moral support. Amicably, he pointed out that if I was going to sit around and wait for my friend for two hours, I might as well write the test, too, just for something to do.

It didn't cost anything, so I did.

A while later, I landed a job with the Ministry of Social Services in Marystown, about three hours away from home. I was part social worker, part financial assistant—at least until someone with a social work degree showed up and took the job. The work was interesting enough, so when I received word that I'd passed the RCMP test and was invited to begin the next stage of the application process, I considered it just my Plan B. (The friend who'd written the test with me also passed, but she had an accident, broke her leg, and was never able to proceed.)

Doing community social services work meant crossing paths with the police. In Marystown, all my encounters with local RCMP were positive. I got to know a married couple—both RCMP officers—and the more I dealt with them, the more the possibility of joining them bloomed in my imagination. The husband, Duncan, was funny and generous. Hanging in a local photography store was a portrait of him with a young boy, both of them dressed in police uniforms. The boy wasn't his son—he belonged to a single mother who lived in the basement apartment of the couple's house—but Duncan had grown so close to the boy that he'd had a very small uniform made.

I requested a ride-along and then another. And I asked a lot of questions. My enthusiasm took over. I caught myself daydreaming about making a difference in the lives of people on both sides of the law, guiding offenders away from crime while helping regular citizens and victims of crime, too. That's when it twigged: policing was exactly the career I wanted. I was young, single, and free to live anywhere, and this was an opportunity I shouldn't pass up.

I threw all my energy into the application process. On a Saturday morning in Harbour Grace, I submitted to fingerprinting for my background check. I stepped out of the police station into the busy downtown street, my fingers still stained with ink, and swore I could hear gossip about my arrest rippling out in all directions.

Later, I gave an in-depth interview. I've seen the notes in my file from that interview:

> A pleasant and articulate individual, she conversed openly throughout the interview and gave the impression of being very sensible and self-confident. The maturity of this applicant exceeds her twenty-two years...excellent recruit material.

Comments about my appearance weave through the report. One reads, "She carries a bit of excess weight but would nevertheless portray a favorable image in uniform." I've always wondered if those comments were made about the male recruits.

On Christmas Eve 1990, I opened the official letter stating that I'd made it through, that I'd been accepted to join the world-renowned Royal Canadian Mounted Police. And I was sick about it. What had I done? What if I hated it? Worse, what if I couldn't do it—what if I made a terrible police officer? The letter mentioned the possibility of a lengthy waiting period based on a weighted selection score, so I grabbed hold of that—a long wait, the chance to get better prepared. I'd already taken up running. I hated it, the running. I cursed every time I pounded the Marystown pavement, trying to suck in enough breath to keep moving. But it was the mental readiness that really concerned me. I wanted to be the best police officer possible. I wanted to serve and protect, and most importantly, I wanted to "Maintain the Right," the words emblazoned in French—*Maintiens le Droit*—on the official insignia. I wanted to make the RCMP proud to have me.

In the end, I didn't have a long wait at all. Just two months later, March 1, 1991, I attended my swearing-in ceremony in a new, navy-blue skirt and blazer over a white blouse. I'd sub-consciously bought the same uniform I'd worn all through school, a look familiar and boring enough to make me feel comfortable.

My parents sat nearby, watching. They must have been proud, but I know they also had their doubts. I sure did.

I signed an oath of allegiance to Her Majesty, Queen Elizabeth II, her heirs and successors according to law.... *So help me God.* I swore that I would faithfully, diligently, and impartially execute and perform the duties required of me as a member of the Royal Canadian Mounted Police, and would well and truly obey all lawful orders and instructions that I received as such, without fear, favor, or affection towards any person.... *So help me God.*

The ceremony went by in a blur, and I only know what was said because my mother kept all the official documents.

After I'd repeated the necessary oaths, the Inspector who performed the ceremony declared: "Pursuant to a delegation of authority by the Commissioner of the Royal Canadian Mounted Police and under paragraph 7(1) (a) of the Royal Canadian Mounted Police Act, I have this day, appointed you: Regular Member." He signed the official document, and I did, too. And just like that, regimental number 43401 was born.

The next day, I packed the items on a list I'd been given, and I caught my flight to Regina, Saskatchewan, to attend the RCMP Depot. All I had to do now was survive basic training.

Standing Tall

2

Another troop mate from Newfoundland and I arrived together at the RCMP training depot in Regina. The Corporal behind the desk asked us where we came from. In unison, we answered, "Newfoundland, Sir!"

And then the Corporal was yelling. "What the hell? You'd better get back on that plane and head back where you came from. We don't want any fucking Newfies here. Goddammit. And don't ever call me sir—I work for a living!"

It took me by surprise like a fast, two-handed shove. I'd heard people on the mainland thought Newfoundlanders weren't as smart or as sophisticated as the rest of the Canadian population, but I held off detailing the many contributions made by people from my part of the country, and in the few seconds it took me to find my balance, I realized the Corporal was kidding. We all laughed. If there's one thing Newfoundlanders have in common, it's that we can take a joke.

The thirty-two members of Troop 27 trickled in over that first day. We came from all across Canada, old and young, men and women. Some followed in their father's footsteps, but many of us were blazing a new trail.

You don't hold back in a situation like this. We clung to each other from the very first day because we knew, whatever came, we would have to go through it together. There were ten other women in my troop—more than I'd expected—and we became fast friends. No personality conflicts, no cliques. We laughed together, cried together, and we helped each other out. After hours, we all sat around in the dorm polishing our gear or cleaning our guns, working on projects, or just talking over the events of the week.

RCMP training was twenty-six weeks of never doing anything right. We were yelled at, we were pushed to the limit, and sometimes we were pushed beyond our limits. And that was fine with me. What better way to prepare a shy girl from Harbour Grace for the high-stress world of policing than months on end of brutish training? They knew every recruit, once out on the street, was going to have to deal regularly with someone raging out of control, so they tested our ability to keep it together. The best thing about Depot was that everybody was treated with the same disrespect to start. Once you showed them you could take it, that you deserved respect, you received it.

I approached the whole process with a fatalistic attitude. I really wanted this, but I knew it might not work out for me. I just needed to know I had given it my all.

My biggest worry—running—turned out to be the least of my concerns. On the very first day at the base, even before training officially began, someone suggested we attempt the "Cooper's run." Cooper's: the final running test at Depot. By the end of training, you had to complete it within a certain time. I was already full of nerves. Now in front of a group of very ambitious people, people I'd known for a few hours, I had to take on Cooper's. I thought I might hyperventilate, but I didn't, and some runners were slower than me. I finished just ten seconds after the time required to graduate.

I could shave ten seconds off that run easily. Relief flooded through me. I had nothing to worry about—not in terms of running, anyway. I'd never be a racehorse. I'd always be somewhere slightly behind the middle of the pack, but that was okay. And of course I knew I could handle the academic tests. Training, it seemed, would be easy.

Except it wasn't all up to me. Everything was a troop effort. If one person was late for class, the rest of us did push-ups until they arrived so they felt pressured to be on time. So we learned fast how to work together for the greater good. If someone was running late, we all stepped in to help them.

Marching drills were even more of a joint effort, a practice to make thirty-two bodies move as one unit. I hated drill. My legs were so short and my paces so small that I struggled to stay in step and cover as much ground as my taller troop mates—and since I stand only five foot three, almost all of them were taller.

One of the biggest sins was going to drill with change in your pocket. If the corporal heard jingling, he would figure out its origin and make that person empty their pockets. He would tell the right marker—the recruit leader for marching—that the culprit owed money to the troop fund. That fund covered costs like our halfway party and dinner for our parents if we made it to graduation, and we all paid into it as punishment. Then he would tell the person with the palm full of coins to pass them over to their right. We'd begin marching again but he would halt us to ask the second person if they had change in their pocket. Of course they did—it had just been given to them. So they, too, were on the hook for a donation, and they too had to pass the change to their neighbour. On and on it went until just about everybody in the troop was fined for having the change.

We studied law in the classroom, did physical and firearms training, and learned self-defence. The fear of being caught cheating was overwhelming. Cheating could get you kicked out, and it wasn't just intentional cheating—accidental cheating was a ticket out, too. If you were ordered to do fifty push-ups or fifty sit-ups and you miscounted, did only forty-eight, you were a cheater. Sometimes another instructor watched from across the gym, counting the reps of a certain recruit. You never knew if it was you, so if you lost count, you did extra—sometimes a lot extra—just to make sure you didn't fall short.

While we were hard at it, our dorms were subject to inspection. Our beds had to be perfectly made; sheets ironed and folded back to exactly the same measurement, corners at a sharp forty-five-degree angle. We used wire clothes hangers to measure the folds. If you screwed it up, you came back at the end of the day to find your bed torn apart and upside down on the floor.

Our closets had to be precisely in order, too, with clothing hung in a certain order. Even the trunks beside our beds could be opened and inspected without notice. We weren't allowed to have any food in our areas, but the girls soon realized we could get away with hiding it in the trunks as long as we lined the top with boxes of tampons, pads, and, for some, birth control. The members doing the inspections were typical men—they could take on the worst of the world, but they wouldn't dream of touching a box of tampons. Underneath, our snacks stayed safe.

Sometimes, in the middle of the night, another troop celebrating their graduation or their halfway mark—a watershed moment in training after which a troop gains some respect—came screaming through the dorm, scaring the crap out of us. Truth is, we couldn't wait for those benchmarks so we could do the exact same thing to some other junior troop.

No matter how tired we were, every morning most of us flew out of bed and scurried to get everything up to inspection standards. One recruit was always up first, frantically tackling her chores and yelling to the rest of us to get up and *haul ass.* Another well-loved girl, Catherine Galliford, always rolled out of bed at the last second and sauntered outside with her tousled bedhead to have a smoke before the day began. After that, she'd perk up and be cheerful and vibrant no matter what the day brought. Together, we all made it to the mess for breakfast on time to meet up with the guys who lived down at the other end of the hall. During the six months we spent together, we all became very close. Any shyness we felt in the beginning turned to solidarity, to allegiance—to just plain getting through it alive.

There were plenty of days when I questioned this career choice. Two decades later, I still have the scars on my knees and my shins from swimming class. The pool was huge and deep, and the water was well below the ledge of the pool deck. If the instructor wanted to punish us (for our sins or just his own bad mood), we had to do "ins and outs." The whole troop would line up along the deep end of the pool. We were each supposed to jump in, push off the pool's bottom, and get right back out again. As the first person hit the water, the second jumped, and then the next and the next, creating a wave pattern of bodies disappearing and reappearing, leaping and clambering. By the time the last person jumped, the first person was supposed to go in again. I'm sure it looked pretty amazing, but there was no slowing down to gape at the spectacle.

I had two problems with ins and outs. I wasn't tall enough to easily touch the bottom and propel myself back up to grab the side of the pool, and the pool's edge was more than the length of my arm from the water. I struggled every time to grab hold and haul myself out. After the second or third time, my knees and shins were skinned from dragging along the tile as I hauled myself up and out. Cut and bleeding, I would stand while the instructor yelled, "Goddammit, Farrell, you're bleeding all over my pool!"

"Yes, Corporal. Sorry, Corporal," was all I was allowed to say.

Other days we had to tread water until our arms felt like they were falling off. And then someone would toss you a brick. It's much harder to tread water when you're clutching a brick, but I held on to that brick for dear life. There was no way I wanted to dive to the deep end's bottom for it. It all sounds crazy and hellish, but those trials imbued me with a tremendous confidence—I knew that if I hadn't drowned in that pool, I wasn't likely to ever go under.

The worst of it, though, was the gas chamber. They tear gassed us so we'd know how it really works, how it chokes and stifles and burns, before we ever chose to use it on someone else. It ensured that if any of us ever had to testify about using it, we could tell the court we knew what that tear gas would do to the people involved. We could say, quite honestly, "Yes, I have experienced it myself."

And it's not an experience you could ever forget. First, they gave us each a cheap sweatsuit to wear and had us run five miles so we were good and sweaty with all our pores wide open. Then they put us into the tear-gas room and made us remove the gas masks they'd issued. We had to breathe in, and we had to answer questions to prove we were breathing. Everything was on fire, my eyes and nose streaming. So much saliva pooled in my throat I almost gagged on it. A lot of people throw up from tear gas. Knowing that, none of us had eaten a thing all day—no one wanted to have to clean up their own puke. Finally, they let us put our gas masks back on, and they taught us to purge them.

Afterward, we were warned to strip down before we entered our dorms so we didn't contaminate everything with tear gas. We'd run a long way on empty stomachs, worked up a sweat, been gassed, and watched each other's reactions. We were just anxious to shower off the day and put it behind us. In the common area outside the doors that led to the women's dorm and the men's dorm, we all shed our clothing right down to our underwear. Nobody cared who saw. We weren't men and women by then, we were just one unit.

On August 26, 1991, the twenty-nine members of Troop 27 who'd made it through graduated from Depot. The women wore skirts and pumps and pillbox hats, and we were one of the last classes issued that female version of the red serge. The ceremony brought a mix of emotions. We were proud, of course, to have gotten through it. Thrilled, actually—and yet...it was our last day together, perhaps forever. Just as we had come from all across Canada, now we were dispersing across the country, heading in different directions, taking what we'd learned to the communities where we'd be posted first.

When assignments were handed out, my name was twinned to Nanaimo. I wasn't even sure what province that was in. The corporal told me to get in my car and drive west until I couldn't go any further, then catch a ferry to Vancouver Island. Ferries and islands—well, I was used to that, anyway, even if I'd be on the absolute opposite end of the country from home.

I went down and bought a car at the Dodge dealership in Regina. There was no going back now.

I took the six o'clock ferry from Vancouver, so it was twilight when I arrived in Nanaimo. Everything seemed beautiful and strange. Leaning on the ferry railing, I was quivering with excitement; disembarking, I was paralyzed with fear. I drove off that ferry a million miles away from my home and my family, from the place where everyone knew me. Here, I was utterly alone. Somebody could kill me, throw me in a ditch, and no one would even realize I was missing—at least until I didn't show up for work the following week.

But my uncertainties didn't extend to my career choice. I was absolutely committed to that. So I made my way to the police station the next day to check in, just to let them know I was ready to start work on schedule. Right away I felt welcomed, gathered in. I felt lucky to get such a great posting.

Committing and Submitting

3

Recruit field training—RFT—lasts about six months, unless your trainer thinks you need more of it. My trainer was an excellent police officer, great with people and especially great for me. Within six weeks I was out on my own.

As in basic training, a new member gets treated with respect only after they've earned it. There's a process of "junior man prove," and I knew with my diminutive stature and Newfoundland accent, I had a lot to prove. New recruits typically don't get sent out on the exciting calls. They don't get to put their recent, excellent training into action until they've cut their teeth on some of the crappier stuff. At first, I attended the kinds of incidents that made me roll my eyes and shake my head. I can remember responding, more than once, to a call from a known drunk who'd made up an emergency just to get a lift somewhere.

New recruits also get pranked, though my turn was much tamer than many I'd witnessed. The watch commander had a loud outburst one night about officers claiming they couldn't find or fit into their formal uniforms anymore, and he ordered everyone on the watch to report to work in red serge the next day. Of course my fellow officers were in on the joke. There I stood in my pumps and pillbox hat at the next shift, listening to everyone else—all of them in regular uniform—hoot with laughter, reminding myself to just let it roll off me.

But not everything was shrugged off easily around the place. Before my time in Nanaimo, another female member had successfully sued the detachment for harassment. Her decision to speak out was deemed unforgivable, and it was never to be forgotten. At watch briefings, we were told to remember "that bitch's name," and if we ever stopped her, to ticket her for whatever we could come up with. This went on for years. Other women had spoken up, too, or had taken action to shut down anyone who got out of line with them. I knew a couple of those women—they were despised around the office.

No one had to explain it to me. As a police officer, your safety depends on the strength of your working relationships. I understood that if I protested sexist behaviour, if I stood up to the office bullies, I could be putting myself at risk. In the RCMP, you do what your superiors tell you to do, and you go where they send you. I feared I would find myself attending a dangerous call alone while a backup car took the scenic route. I didn't want to get beaten—or worse—and then have a colleague slyly remind me that my attitude, my bitchiness, was to blame.

Of course the vast majority of police officers are dedicated to looking out for each other. They had my back on the road and in personal ways, too. Once, when someone was trying to set me up with another young, single officer, a colleague who worked in Victim Services stood behind the would-be matchmaker and shook her head madly, used her finger to mimic slitting her own throat and shooting herself in the temple. I got the message: this probably wasn't the fellow for me.

I learned early which men to stay away from. Even after I'd

earned my place with the majority of members in my detachment, there were those who would never approve of a female officer—and maybe, especially, a short woman—but I could live with that. I loved my job. I didn't need them to talk to me or to acknowledge my equality. I figured they were just the last vestiges of a dying breed in a changing world.

Later, though, I noticed something. Those members were the same ones who concurred with management on everything. They were the ones who got promoted.

WHEN I ARRIVED IN NANAIMO, there was one member on the management team who was obviously an alcoholic. He would come to work drunk and take the police car out on the road. It was not uncommon for him to call into work and claim he couldn't remember where he had parked his vehicle the day or night before. Then the dispatcher would ask us all to keep an eye out for the car. It always turned up.

Everybody in the detachment knew, and everybody laughed about it. But underneath the laughter there was something else: dread. Because there was always the chance you would be the one called to the accident—you would be the one to see first-hand the wreckage when this officer finally injured or killed someone on the road. And then you'd have to decide how to deal with it.

The RCMP has an image of honour and integrity to maintain. It claims its members are the cream of the crop, that only the best get hired. If you arrested your superior, you'd embarrass the RCMP and become, forever, a known rat among your peers. The only other option would be to lie, to chalk the accident up to some other cause, maintain the facade that RCMP officers were upright and above reproach—and maintain the respect of your peers and your supervisors. But if you lied, could you live with it? You would have to hope the public never found out that you'd fudged your report, hope you never had to look the victims of the accident in the eye.

Somehow, thank God, it never happened. There was no accident, but there were mortifying instances when this supervisor came to back me up at calls and was so intoxicated he could hardly stand without wavering. Everyone on the scene had to know he was drunk. He reeked of booze, got back into his car, and drove away. And I let him, every time. I didn't know what else to do. How could I intervene when those in the office who were far superior to me wouldn't? I was, quite frankly, afraid of the consequences if I arrested this officer for impaired driving. And then I feared I was every bit as much responsible because I took no action.

The sergeant was a nice man, drunk or sober, and he probably died years before his time from the complications of alcoholism. In the period I worked with him, I never saw any evidence that our organization tried to help him, that anyone in the RCMP did anything more than chuckle about his problem. Maybe they did—maybe they tried and he refused help. I don't know, but I do know that for the safety of the public and for his own safety, he should have been taken off the road until he got sober.

None of us did that for him.

ALL OF THE CALLS, EMERGENCY or not, were received in the radio room in the core of the RCMP building. The employees who answered those calls and dispatched them were mainly civilian members and mostly women. And they were delightful. When it was quiet and there was time, it was common for female police officers to hang out in the radio room and listen to the chat. I found it far more appealing than sitting out in the bull pit, listening to the veteran officers boast about all their accomplishments. In the radio room, there was a familiar rhythm of female conversation that allowed me to relax, to let my guard down.

Syd was one of the older dispatchers, and she was like the matriarch of the group. Her calm demeanor and ability to multitask revealed her years of experience in the radio room. She liked to mother the incoming recruits. It was comforting, with my family so far away, to slide under the wing of this amazing woman.

One day Syd called my attention to a young municipal employee, Wayne, a caretaker in our building. She said he was a sweetheart and asked if I'd met him. I had seen him around, but I'd been far too busy with my RFT to pay attention to much else. Syd just told me to keep my eye on him, and because I trusted her, I did. Soon, I was noticing him everywhere, and finally, we struck up a conversation. I told him I was trying to get settled in, and he told me he had a truck if I needed to get any furniture.

A few days later, he asked me to tag along for his usual Wednesday night drink with his buddy, Bob. Out for a drink in the middle of the week? That set off my warning bells. I didn't drink, and I wasn't interested in watching other people drink, so I declined. He asked again another week, and again I said no. And I would have kept saying no, but Syd intervened, told me I just had to go out with him. The next time he brought it up, I asked him where they went every Wednesday.

"Tim Horton's."

"What? I thought you went to a bar for a drink?"

Wayne laughed. "Oh God no. Neither of us drinks. We just go for a coffee and a bullshit."

Of course I went along, and I met Bob. They had grown up together and were great friends, and we all hit it off. One coffee date turned into many, and for a little while, I began to think I was dating both Wayne and Bob. But soon, my friendship with

Wayne blossomed into a great romance and, within months, became something we could both see as permanent.

I lived in a high-rise in downtown Nanaimo. Wayne had a little house on Duke Street in the old neighbourhood where he'd grown up. We took turns visiting each other, but we were keeping our relationship a secret around the office. That way, if it didn't work out, nobody would ever know.

Wayne Merlo was a single, caring man from a good family. That was a big part of his appeal. He was also the only son, an adopted son, in an Italian family. Wayne's dad, Jack (Giovanni), was a hardworking man. Raised on a dairy farm, he left home as a young teen to pursue work in the coal mines of Vancouver Island. That's where he met Kathleen Drake, a pretty, young chambermaid working in a motel north of Nanaimo. After their daughter Jeannie was born, Jack switched to the logging camps, then applied for a job at the local pulp mill, Harmac. Those were the days before formal résumés. When the interviewer asked how much schooling he had, Jack said that he had "half grade twelve." That was pretty good for his generation. Satisfied, the boss gave Jack the job. Jack put in twenty-five years at Harmac, and he never admitted he had only a grade six education—grade six, *half* of twelve.

Wayne's parents were in their sixties when I met them. They'd been married for a very long time and were obviously still in love. His mom was just recovering from a heart attack, a quadruple bypass, and a leg amputation. She'd been to hell and back, but always had a smile and never complained.

I remember thinking that if he was raised by such a wonderful family, by this strong woman and a man who cared so much for his wife, then I couldn't go wrong.

And anyway, Wayne was my version of prince charming. He was handsome with dark hair that would have curled if he'd let it grow longer. He was tall and fit, and for a long time, I wasn't quite sure what he saw in a short thing like me. And better yet, Wayne was tidy. In fact, he was very tidy for a bachelor who lived on his own. An older lady once came to his door to solicit a donation for charity, and after she stepped inside, she kept asking him if he really lived alone. She claimed she'd never met a tidier man. But it made sense. He was, after all, a custodian at the police station back then. He liked cleaning up, keeping things orderly, and I didn't complain. What woman would complain about a tidy man?

WHEN YOU RUN A VEHICLE through the police computer system to do a check, you can print up a hard copy for your file. I got to work one day and found, in my drawer, a printout of vehicle information I hadn't run. It was Wayne's vehicle information, his plate number, and the location of the vehicle when the query was done: outside a downtown high-rise at three in the morning.

Busted.

One of my colleagues was watching as I opened my drawer. I looked up to see him smiling. "Is there anything you want to tell me?" I knew he'd already put two and two together.

And it wasn't the only time one of our cars gave us away. Wayne's mother, Kay, got a phone call from one of Wayne's neighbours, a lady she'd known since their children were growing up. The call came right out of the blue, and the woman began to talk about raising children, about how you just have to hope they make good choices, and about how hard it is to worry about them. Wayne's mom had no idea why the conversation was taking this turn—especially since all of their children had grown up and moved out. When Kay tried to get off the phone, the lady blurted, "Oh for God's sake, Kay, I have to tell you. I'm not sure what Wayne is doing over in that house, but there's a cop car there every other day. I thought you should know!"

Our relationship, it seemed, was determined to come out in

the open. But we were confident by that time, sure of what was between us, so we decided it was time to tell everyone.

We didn't anticipate the danger of doing so.

Not long after we came out as a couple, Wayne and I had an argument that turned nasty when Wayne accused me of having slept with another RCMP officer. I was stunned. And furious. I hardly knew the guy. I couldn't believe Wayne would accuse me like that.

But there was a simple explanation for why he thought I had. The officer had approached Wayne and asked, "Are you seeing Janet Farrell?" When Wayne said yes, the man replied, "I fucked her, too."

It was common around the detachment, this puffed-up boasting about having had sex with the new girl.

One of my supervisors also felt the need to mention to Wayne, maybe as a means of congratulations, that I was the perfect girlfriend—just the right height for giving a blow job with a beer balanced on my head.

I refused to be overly sensitive. I never wanted the men to feel like they had to watch their language around me. I liked it when they told a good, off-colour joke in my presence because it meant they were comfortable with me, that I had succeeded in becoming one of the guys. When I went into that same supervisor's office to drop off my paperwork for his approval at the end of shift, he often asked me to stand beside the naked blow-up doll he was renowned for keeping in his office. He wanted to see how I measured up. I was an officer in uniform trying to learn the ropes, focusing all my energy and attention on becoming a credible, reliable police officer, yet at the end of a long shift, I was supposed to cozy up to the boss's sex toy. I didn't do it. I always found a way to redirect the conversation back to the files and then get the hell out of the room without going near that doll. I figured I had joined a predominantly male organization and that some behaviour just went with the territory, but having to deal with it meant that instead of having some genuine trust and rapport with my supervisor, I approached his office with the same trepidation I felt attending a potentially dangerous call.

The blow-up doll was dispiriting, but finding out one of the members was claiming to have slept with me? That was both infuriating and isolating. It crossed a line. It said I wasn't one of the guys, that I was something else. Something they could use and toss aside. Something different, cheap, and not equal at all.

Fortunately, Wayne believed me when I told him I'd never been with that man, and we never talked about it again. Neither of us had the power at the detachment to confront it head on, so we pushed it aside, though for a long time after, whenever I saw my lying co-worker, I felt anger rise like bile in my throat.

A CALL CAME IN OVER the radio that an officer had attempted to pull over a vehicle, but the driver had refused to stop. The car was northbound on Howard Avenue, and I was close by, on Jingle Pot Road heading south. I responded, heading fast to the area to get involved in what might become a pursuit or even a high-speed chase—my first, and I wanted to be part of it. Other cars also responded, racing to the area to cut off the offending vehicle. As the suspect turned off Howard onto Jingle Pot Road, he lost control and launched the car off the road and into one of the thickest blackberry patches the city had to offer.

Police cars converged. Officers ran to pull the suspect from his vehicle. It was a teenage boy, maybe fifteen or sixteen years old and thankfully unhurt. As soon as he was handcuffed, he fell face down into that thicket of blackberry brambles. He was wailing, yelling, "You got me. You got me!"

I wasn't down there. I'd stayed up on the side of the road; there were more than enough officers in the ditch to deal with a teenager face down in the brambles, hands cuffed behind his back. But I could make out his cries: "You got me!" And I could clearly hear and see the hitting and the kicking when it began.

None of us at that scene knew what, if anything, this kid had done wrong other than refusing to stop for police, but I knew one thing for sure: nothing warranted being beaten while face down in a thick torture of blackberry bushes by law enforcement officers. Later, I would wonder if the boy had a friend with a similar story, a friend who served as a warning to him, that convinced this young man not to trust the police and not to stop when he saw the flashing lights.

There were a few of them laying on the blows, but the most serious assault wasn't committed by a hired and trained police officer. It was an auxiliary officer, a volunteer, and one of the most respected auxiliary officers we had.

Tears filled my eyes as I stood above that ditch with the red and blue lights from our cars illuminating the darkness. Every single member at that scene had more seniority than I did. I was so junior, and I was thinking, "How can this be happening? Those people down there are RCMP, sworn to serve and protect just like me."

But in that instance, I did neither serve nor protect. I just turned away. I went back to my car, climbed inside, and I cried.

I knew if that kid launched a complaint, the attending members who'd been down in the ditch would say he'd resisted arrest. They would never admit the suspect was already handcuffed, down on the ground and yelling, "You got me!" As long as everyone stuck together, as long as every officer who'd responded to the call told the same story, they would have no trouble being believed over some kid who didn't stop for the police.

Hunched over the wheel in my cruiser, wiping away tears of shock and grief, I asked myself what I would do. Would I be a rat, report the assault I'd witnessed to my direct supervisor—a man who had already deemed me good blow-job height? Would I file a formal complaint on behalf of a teenager who was probably too afraid to speak out? No, I would not. I was so junior, but even that early in my career, I understood there was no one to tell. In a paramilitary organization, order is maintained by mute force—you just don't speak out against those who outrank you. That's how order is maintained.

But I told myself that if that boy did launch a complaint, I would tell the truth. I would back him up, stand up for him with every ounce of integrity I still had. I would provide a statement and live with the fallout.

That night, I resolved within myself that, while I would not break the silence, I would never lie.

When I left that roadside, I was forever changed. There were, of course, other members at the scene who had no part in the assault. But since they never spoke about it and I didn't either, I don't know if any of them carried the same heavy shame, if the silence was slowly eating them up inside.

As for that auxiliary officer, though he continued with the detachment for years, I never took him out in my car after that.

WAYNE BECAME MY OFFICIAL VANCOUVER Island tour guide. Every time we had a day off together, we chose a different destination. He'd check on his mother first—he worried about her constantly—and off we'd go. Together, we marvelled at the beautiful, massive Douglas fir trees of Cathedral Grove and the thundering ocean waves of Pacific Rim National Park. We camped in his old Ford pickup truck, sleeping in the back under the canopy and roughing it.

On our first trip to Salt Spring Island, just a short ferry ride away, we went to the amazing crafters market in the center of the main town, Ganges. It was a gorgeous fall day, and we hung out on the waterfront and perused the market. In a little hardware store, I finally found a big Maglite flashlight, the kind police officers like to carry because they're bright and sturdy, and they last. I'd looked everywhere in Nanaimo for one, but hadn't been successful. I still have that flashlight from Ganges. It's been useful, and more importantly, it has served as a reminder of that very happy time when Wayne and I were just starting out.

It was in a hotel room in Victoria that Wayne proposed to me. We'd travelled down for a couple of days. Early in the morning, we were watching TV when a commercial about a couple advertising their real-estate services from their limousine struck us as hilarious. Wayne started imitating the commercial, poking fun at it, and then we were both laughing, and out of the blue, Wayne asked me to marry him. He hadn't planned the moment—there was no fancy dinner or scenic outlook. It was just the right moment. I admired that about him, his spontaneity.

I said yes, of course. And I was thrilled—I could just imagine how much fun we'd enjoy in our life together.

I'D WANTED CHILDREN FOR AS long as I could remember—I was the kind of girl who nurtured her dolls and took the neighbour's babies for walks—but I didn't want them until I was able to make a good life for them, until I found someone who would embrace parenthood with me. There was nothing Wayne wanted more than to have a baby, too, and to have that baby soon, while his mother was still around to meet her grandchild. Kay had been told not to expect more than about two years out of life by her doctor after they'd amputated her leg due to circulatory problems. She was vocal about wanting to see Wayne settled and happy with a family of his own.

On a Friday night in May, I was scheduled to work, but I was doubled over with abdominal pain. I already suspected I was pregnant and had told Wayne, but we hadn't even had it confirmed by a doctor. Wayne rushed me to the hospital. The first diagnosis was a tubal pregnancy—I'd lose the baby and the tube and an ovary. I was devastated. Then a specialist arrived and quickly determined I was having an appendicitis attack. While the surgery put my early pregnancy at risk, there was still a chance the baby would be okay.

When I returned to work, one of the members cornered me and asked how I was. He wasn't a man known for his compassion and concern. In fact, most of us thought he was a ladder-climbing jerk, one of those rule followers who rose through the ranks by memorizing the manual but whose condescending attitude toward the public kept him from ever being an effective police officer. He gave me the smug grin he was famous for and said he'd heard about my abortion.

Here I was, worried sick about whether my baby would survive the anesthetic I'd had to have and he wanted to stir the pot, start a rumour that I'd had an abortion. Since Wayne and I weren't telling anyone I was pregnant until I'd made it through the first trimester, I had to keep my voice steady and my outrage under control, so I didn't blurt it out. In as steady a voice as I could muster, I told him it was just my appendix I'd had removed. He grinned again and assured me he knew the truth—but he was willing to keep my little secret.

For months, up until I made our news public, every time I saw that member he would wink and give me a sly grin, like he had something on me. And I would glare silently at him and have to content myself with the thought of how stupid he'd feel when he heard the truth.

RCMP BOSSES USUALLY KEEP THEIR doors open; members are free to come and go. When you see a closed door, you know somebody on the other side is in trouble. You scan the office to see who's missing. Then your stomach starts to churn as you wonder if you're next.

My first closed-door session took me completely by surprise. After all, I didn't think I had done anything wrong.

My pregnancy had survived those first uncertain months, and I'd gone to talk to my doctor about being taken off the road. There comes a time when wearing the heavy gun belt and going on calls, risking the safety of your unborn child, is just not worth it. A doctor's note could get a pregnant member re-assigned to office duty. Although I knew it was the right choice for me and for the well-being of my new family, it's not always easy to put your personal life ahead of your responsibility as a police officer. I felt guilty, not being able to pull my full weight for a while, not being able to give my all for my watch mates. Still, it felt necessary and right.

Doctor's note in hand, nervous as hell, I headed upstairs to the operational officer's second-floor office. He was a stern man, not given to friendly chit-chat, but I made small talk anyway for a few minutes before I worked up the courage to tell him the reason I was there.

I don't remember if he closed the door or if he told me to do it.

I sat across the desk from him, nervously watching as he read the doctor's note confirming my pregnancy. Then he raised his eyes and glowered at me. Finally, he spoke, and even though I'd anticipated the worst, what he said was far worse than anything I could have expected.

"What am I supposed to do with you now?"

I didn't answer. I didn't understand the question because I didn't yet know that the RCMP had no plan for dealing with pregnant members. His voice deepened when he asked again, "What the fuck am I supposed to do with you now?"

Then he began to shout at me, louder and louder while my

stomach churned and my head swam. I felt like I was being pummeled, like there was a fist pressing deep into my guts. His diatribe finally ended with this charge: "You had better decide what you are going to do with your life! You're either going to have a career in the RCMP or you're going to pop out kids."

I still hadn't said anything. I was in shock, blindsided by his rage. I got up and headed for the door. I could feel the tears coming, the contents of my stomach roiling up. I had delivered my doctor's note; there was no point in trying to say anything, in trying to defend my choice to become a parent. As I fled, he delivered the final blow. "I have a suggestion for you—next time, keep your fucking legs closed!"

I pulled the door shut behind me and tore off to the washroom. As I violently threw up, I wondered if the whole office had heard that humiliating, lengthy admonishment, if I would be a pariah now in my own detachment.

Wayne and I planned to marry in the fall, smack in the middle of my pregnancy. I was still wearing my regular uniform, hadn't crossed into maternity clothes yet, but no way was I walking down the aisle in my red serge. Wayne was marrying Janet the woman, not Janet the police officer. I figured getting married in uniform was, for the male officers, more than a point of pride; it was also a way to avoid having to rent a tux or buy a new suit. But like all brides, I wanted to be beautiful.

I didn't need anything fancy and frothy; I just wanted something feminine that fit right. And it wasn't easy to find. Wedding dresses were made for taller women—women whose bodies weren't already shape-shifting to accommodate a baby—and nothing worked on me. Wayne's only sister, Jeannie, years his senior and mine, was quickly becoming the sister I never had. She came with me on my dress search, and eventually, we made a trip down to Victoria, where we exhausted every bridal store in the city and my optimism, too. Finally, we turned into a little downtown shop that seemed to have more knick-knacks and souvenirs than anything else, but on a wall in the back, Jeannie spotted some wedding dresses. Among them was a lovely, lace dress in my size. It fit like it had been made for me. Plus, it was on sale. I remember feeling like there'd been a divine intervention, like destiny was smiling on me and Wayne and our shared future.

My faith, however, did not smile. Since Wayne's family didn't practice any organized religion, I had gone to a Catholic church in Nanaimo to arrange the ceremony. But there was a snag. Wayne had been married before, years before, when he was very young. After a few years, he and his young wife had realized they wanted different things. There were no children involved, so the divorce was simple and amicable. Wayne always spoke very highly of his ex, who had moved to the mainland after their split.

When the priest learned about Wayne's previous marriage, he told us there was only one way to make it right. Wayne would have to go to a lawyer, locate his ex-wife, and, with her co-operation, have the paperwork switched from a divorce to an annulment. If it appeared Wayne's marriage had been annulled, we would be allowed to get married in the Catholic Church. Wayne had no qualms about approaching his ex and no doubt that she would sign any papers we asked, but he didn't want to deny the marriage had existed. Neither of us liked being asked to lie. It just didn't sit right, the idea that a divorce decree was grounds for the church to refuse to marry us, but papering over the divorce with a fraudulent annulment made it okay in their eyes and, I guess they believed, in God's eyes, too.

We walked away from the Catholic Church and instead had a small ceremony at the Anglican Church where they welcomed two strangers and, because we were law-abiding people who wanted to pledge our lives to one another, married us with all the respect they would have shown lifetime parishioners. And so for years after, whenever we heard the bells ring there, Wayne would smile and exclaim, "That's our church!"

Small was perfect. I never wanted a big wedding, and I hate being the centre of attention. There were just twenty-two people in attendance. With both of us working at the police station, Wayne and I knew if we invited one person, we would have to invite all two-hundred employees in the building. Why did I need a bunch of men I hardly knew standing guard in their red serge at my wedding? Besides, I wanted my personal life to stay separate from my work life. So we invited just our families and our closest friends. My parents flew out from Newfoundland for the wedding—they had come to visit the spring before, too, to meet Wayne—and though they would have much preferred the wedding to precede the pregnancy, they were as supportive as their culture and their Catholic upbringing allowed.

My dad walked me down the aisle, and my mother—my best friend—served as my maid of honour. I felt beautiful, blessed, and very happy.

After that closed door session, I don't think I ever looked the operational officer in the eye again. I would lower my head in shame every time I saw him. I was a healthy young woman expecting her first baby, but I felt beaten down, demoralized. My excitement was overlaid by dread as I anticipated what the next few months would bring. Of course many of our colleagues were thrilled for us—Syd, who was taking great pride in her matchmaking skill, organized a baby shower. But others just couldn't keep their derisive comments to themselves. I would occasionally hear a remark like, "Sure is busy out there today. Janet could take some calls if she wasn't knocked up." The tone was meant to belittle, and it worked. I was doing my best to contribute to the detachment, but the office duties I was asked to perform were mostly just odd jobs. There wasn't really much use for me.

I was, I think, only the second female member to get pregnant in that detachment. The RCMP had been hiring women since 1974, and by the early 1990s women accounted for more than eight percent of regular members. Still, the management in my area had somehow failed to consider a strategy for making good use of pregnant members. Even the maternity uniform was a joke—a giant three-man tent I only pretended to order. It was as if the old boys' club just couldn't quite grasp the idea of women among the ranks, let alone women members who wanted children. Ironically, the male officers in the detachment were, for the most part, married and having children—or their wives were having children, anyway.

Five years later, Bev Busson—one of the first women Mounties and the only woman ever to serve as Commissioner of the RCMP—presented at a workshop on women in policing in Canada. She declared that the practice of not backfilling for maternity leave (or paternity leave, which was much less common then) caused additional stress to other members who had to work with fewer officers on duty, and led to tension and resentment. The same concern was raised in the 2006 Employment Systems Review.

And so what should have been a joyous time for me was instead a period of intense distress. Maternity leave couldn't come soon enough, and though we very much wanted more than one child, I figured we'd have to wait a long time before I dared get pregnant again.

WAYNE'S FRIEND, BOB, HAD FOUND a truck he wanted to buy at a local dealership, but he wanted Wayne to take a look at it before he committed. Easy enough, except that Bob worked days and Wayne worked evenings, so it was almost midnight when we picked up Bob and headed for the dealership. I went along. I couldn't have cared less about the truck, but I was nine months pregnant, as wide as I was tall, and restless. Any outing was a distraction from the discomfort of waiting.

The truck Bob wanted was parked at the back of the lot. He had come prepared with flashlights, so we all took one and shined our beams on the truck. Wayne and Bob looked inside, checked out the box, and did what guys do when talking to each other about a truck. None of us gave a thought to the new policing section that had started up in Nanaimo, plainclothes officers conducting overnight patrols to combat property crime in the most targeted areas of town.

After a while, we made our way back through the dark lot to Wayne's old beater Toyota Corolla. Bob climbed into the backseat—my belly was so big, I couldn't fit back there—and off we went, heading southbound toward Bob's place. As we approached a set of traffic lights, we saw the red and blue flashers of a police car behind us. Wayne was sure one of the officers from work had recognized his little beater and was just saying hello. He stopped at the intersection and planned to move through it on the green and then pull over. But when the light changed and we began to move, we heard shouting. Wayne stopped the car. Suddenly there was an undercover police officer with his gun to my head at the passenger-door window, yelling for me to "get out of the fucking car." I turned toward him, rolled down my window part way—I was too alarmed to crank it all the way down—and screamed, "What the hell are you doing?"

When he saw who it was, I'm not sure who was more scared. He put his gun away and, in an excited stammer, began to explain that he'd seen our old car and the flashlights and naturally assumed someone was breaking into vehicles at the dealership.

I didn't give a shit what he'd assumed—it wasn't a good enough reason to draw a gun and hold it to somebody's head. Seething, I pointed out that if he'd panicked and pulled the trigger, he would have shot a nine-month-pregnant co-worker. He didn't know what to say. He had to be afraid that we'd make an official report and get him in a lot of trouble. I was almost concerned enough to do it, too, because the incident alarmed me. How many other times had he pulled his gun on an unsuspecting member of the public for a relatively minor incident?

After we explained about conflicting work schedules and Bob's need to show Wayne his new truck, we all had a laugh. I never did lay a complaint—he was a good officer, fair and well-respected. If he was a little overly anxious, a little too quick to draw, at least he knew how to stand down.

And now I knew something I hadn't known before: I knew how it felt to look down the business end of a gun barrel.

Giving Too Much Away

4

In January 1993, I gave birth to a healthy baby girl with a full head of curly dark hair. We named her Ashley, and I threw myself into motherhood with the same commitment I had shown in school, in university, in training, and in my career. I truly enjoyed the traditional female roles, and I was determined to excel as a mother and a wife. I was equally determined to shine as a police officer. I believed so strongly in the need for women police officers and in the importance of the female perspective in the field. It never occurred to me that I couldn't play all these roles and do them well. It was just going to require a strong commitment.

It wasn't long before I realized that a lot of people didn't share the same sense of commitment. Their desire to rise in the ranks of the RCMP surpassed their desire to serve and protect the community. Some members would sacrifice anything, including their integrity, for a promotion. Not all of them, of course, but too many of them.

And frankly, it's understandable. Promotion through the ranks—not being a good police officer—is what counts as a sign of success in the RCMP. Men whose fathers were also members felt intense pressure to reach the same rank and then, preferably, get the promotion that allowed them to outrank the old man.

Ironically, the lowest rank in the RCMP, the constable, has the greatest impact. Constables are the backbone of the RCMP and account for the highest percentage of frontline policing. They are the first responders, the ones who attend robberies, accidents, suicides, domestic disturbances, and any number of other tragedies, large and small. They are overworked, underpaid, and bogged down in paperwork. Out in public, they face constant criticism. I couldn't possibly recount all the snide remarks that came my way, but I can clearly remember stopping at a coffee shop to pick up something hot for someone cold and homeless I'd just dealt with and overhearing, behind me, a comment about a lazy pig in the donut shop.

I WAS CALLED TO A local department store late one afternoon after the loss prevention officer caught three teenage girls stealing make-up. He detained them. When I arrived, I explained to the girls the reason for their arrest and advised them of their rights. Then I looked through their purses—standard procedure—to see if they'd taken anything else. In the second purse, I found a baggie full of what was obviously marijuana. The theft of a four-dollar lip gloss had suddenly escalated to possession of a controlled substance for one sobbing girl.

I put all three into the back of the car and told them I was taking them home. We'd have a talk with their parents and decide where to go from there. The girl facing a drug charge was the most upset, of course. She had the most to worry about.

The parents of the girl who had been the quietest, the most deferential, reacted just as you hope all parents will. They were respectful of me and angry with their daughter, but obviously supportive of her as well. They made it very clear they didn't approve of her actions, and they hoped getting arrested would curb any similar behavior. They said they would support any consequences that came her way, but added that she was a good student, and they hoped a criminal record wouldn't hurt her future prospects. I assured them we could work something out and headed back to my car with some faith in the world.

It was a different story at the other two houses. One girl's parents were enraged the moment they opened the door. But it wasn't their daughter they were mad at. When I explained their daughter had been caught shoplifting, they started to yell. How dare I embarrass them by coming to their home? What was I thinking? Why didn't I just call and have them pick her up? Now the neighbours would talk. They proceeded to call me stupid, to tell me that they were both doctors—*doctors!*—and I had embarrassed them by bringing a cop car to their home. If you have nothing better to do than arrest thirteen-year-old girls for stealing lipstick, one said, obviously our tax dollars aren't well spent. They trotted out that common slur—*we* pay *your* salary—and they threatened to lodge a complaint with my boss. They told me to get the hell out of their house.

In a situation like that, you can't give what you get. You have to stay calm. I gave them my name and the file number and told them I'd be in touch about the theft. They said they'd get the best lawyer possible to fight this "bullshit," because their daughter was going to have a bright future and do more with her life than I'd done with mine. Then they slammed the door in my face.

Back in the car, marijuana girl was still hysterical. I'd already told her I might be able to find some alternative to laying a charge if she would work with me, tell me who had supplied her with drugs. She didn't want to disclose her source, but as we neared her house, the hysteria escalated. I pulled over and opened the window that separated me from the back seat. Respect mattered, even with kids—maybe especially with kids—and I tried to imagine how I'd want someone to approach the matter if my daughter were in this situation. I explained the seriousness of her predicament, and as I talked, she calmed down, listened, nodded. Once again I asked her to tell me where she got that marijuana.

"From my mom's nightstand drawer. She's going to kill me when she finds out I took her drugs."

I knew right then I wasn't going to get a warm reception at this house, either.

Mom was angrier that her pot had been seized than she was about the shoplifting. She said her daughter was a good kid and if the department stores didn't "jack the prices of the fucking make-up so high, kids wouldn't be forced to steal it."

Finally, she said, "Thanks for bringing her home. I've had a couple of beers. I couldn't drive over to get her at the mall."

CONSTABLES ARE DERIDED WITHIN THE organization every bit as much as they are in the community. Members who don't pursue the promotional path, who stay by choice at the level of first responder, are scoffed at by other RCMP. CFL—Constable For Life—is a derogatory term. If you want to avoid being doomed to derision, you have to build your career. Often that means brown-nosing, doing favours that have nothing to do with the job, ratting out disliked co-workers for small infractions, and spending your time looking busy in front of supervisors instead of getting out and doing the hard work. Too many years as a constable become a black eye, not an asset. In my experience, those who'd logged the longest time in the trenches, taking the calls, made the best managers because they'd spent years honing their problem solving skills. But if you weren't willing to do the dance of the peacocks, you weren't going anywhere.

I wasn't willing to dance, and my career path was never going to be meteoric.

I just loved hands-on policing way too much. I loved patrolling the streets, working in the community, meeting a great wide range of people, and coming to understand that although we were so diverse individually, we shared a common humanity, a set of characteristics that we held in different balances. And I loved getting to know people like Fred.

Fred was a typical drug addict who hung out with typical druggie types and had a girlfriend who was also an addict. Nothing unusual there. But then she got pregnant and Fred had a daughter, and suddenly, he had a good reason to get clean. Once he'd been clean for a while, he won custody of his toddler from the mother who wasn't able to clean up her act. It was all working out okay until, out pushing his little girl's stroller, he ran into a dealer who suddenly remembered that Fred owed him money. There'd been a dust up on the street, and that's how I came to be involved.

Fred was desperate to stay on the road to recovery, to keep his little girl, and to keep her safe. He wanted a no contact order, and I helped him with that. In the weeks that followed, I saw Fred quite often, out walking with his daughter, always beaming. He was like the poster boy for overcoming addiction and adversity.

I always stopped to have a chat with them. I had a little girl about the same age, so I wasn't surprised when Fred's daughter told me she liked Beanie Babies. I wanted them both to know the community was on their side, so on Christmas Eve I left a gift of Beanie Babies hanging on their doorknob late at night.

Later, Fred went back to school and became a successful chef, and he raised his daughter as a single dad. The last time I ran into him—not long after I'd had to leave the RCMP—she was a teenager. Fred was so proud of her, and I was reminded that determined people can move forward, can salvage a good life out of even the most desperate circumstances.

One of the most important tools a police officer carries is her notebook. It contains every day, every shift, and every call. When you start a shift, you note the date and the zone in which you're working. On a call, you document the time, the location, and the names of those you spoke with and anything else that could be relevant. You keep a brief and accurate record, knowing the page numbers have been pre-printed in every bottom corner so it would be obvious if anything was torn out. Sometimes you write about the weather or jot down other details to help jog your memory later. When you place someone under arrest, you read them their rights, ensure they understand those rights, and then you document their acknowledgement. That way, when you appear in court eighteen months later and the accused says they were never advised of their rights, you can refer to your notebook and refute their claim.

I still have dozens of notebooks with the start and end dates written on the front cover, all of them brimming with stories. Those stories are like a compendium on human nature, on the way different people react to events.

In 1997, I attended a theft complaint. A number of silk plants had been taken from the main foyer of a condominium building. The woman who'd called it in was inconsolable. The building committee had just spent a lot of money on those plants, and now thieves had breached the lobby of what the residents had believed was a safe building. The woman was beside herself about it. I wanted to point out that they were just silk plants for heaven's sake, not her grandmother's wedding ring, but it was hardly my place to question her feelings. I had a job to do, and I treated her and her complaint with respect. When I left the building, she was still very upset.

On the same day, members working in a different part of town were called in because a woman hadn't seen her neighbour in a few days. He lived on the other side of her duplex, and his mail and newspapers were beginning to pile up. Since he always let her know when he was going away, she was worried. It's known as a "check the welfare of" call, and they are common.

The officers saw the neighbour's car in the garage, and they found the owner inside it. He had rigged up a hose to the exhaust pipe and died in the driver's seat. The weather had been hot, and a couple of days had gone by, so the smell was overpowering. But what my colleagues couldn't get over was the reaction of the lady who'd called it in. She came into the garage, looked into the car, saw her neighbour in a rapid state of decomposition just a few metres from her home, and her response was, "Yup, that's him." Then she went off to tackle her day.

BUT THERE ARE FUNNY STORIES too, and stories that highlight just how often criminals catch themselves. I responded when a woman called to say she had some information on an armed robbery that had occurred a few days prior at a local beer and wine store. The suspect had been caught on video; the video had aired on the evening news.

She let me into her apartment. Her brother was there too, and he seemed surprised by my arrival. She quickly fingered him as the suspect, saying, "I gave him that hoodie for Christmas, and that's my hat he was wearing in that video on the news."

I don't know who looked more shocked—the suspect whose sister had just ratted him out or me because I was face to face with an armed-robbery suspect with no backup.

He called her a liar, denied the charge. I managed to convince him that I believed him but had to follow procedure, take him downtown, and do some preliminary investigation. I advised him of his rights, and he came willingly, eager to show his sister was lying. But she had produced the hoodie and the hat, and we were able to gather enough evidence to lay a charge. Throughout the entire process, he maintained his innocence.

Months passed. The trial date was approaching when we got a call to attend an apartment building where a man had kicked in the second-floor door. He'd come to beat up the man inside because he thought the guy had stolen something from his mother. To escape an imminent and probably severe beating, the alleged thief had jumped off the second floor balcony. But he didn't land so well, so along with the police, there was an ambulance on the scene.

As the paramedics strapped him securely to the stretcher, I recognized him as the alleged armed robber from months before. "Hey, how are ya buddy? I haven't seen you in months."

He looked over and recognized me. "I'm doing well, thank you, ma'am. I've been really good since I did that armed robbery."

I smiled. An admission after all this time. "I'll just enter that into my notebook and forward it to the Crown for court next week," I told him. The paramedics were my witnesses, and all the poor guy could do, laying there on that stretcher, was yell "Fuck!"

Within a couple of days, I received notice that the armed robbery trial had been cancelled. The suspect had pled guilty.

POLICE OFFICERS JOKE ABOUT COUNTING down the number of "shoplifting days" until Christmas. Thefts peak as people try to live up to the expectations of what they think they must give, and break-ins escalate because thieves know most homes are loaded with expensive new things—new, packaged, and often with the receipt—all tucked away in one spot.

A notebook reminded me of an older woman I met one year just before Christmas. When I arrived at her house, her eyes were red from crying. She'd gone to the nursing home to visit her mother, who was more than 100 years old, that afternoon and returned to find the nasty mess of a break in.

In her hallway closet, thieves had discovered the Christmas gifts she'd wrapped and put away for her grandchildren and her great-grandchildren. They didn't stop at ripping off the wrapping paper to see what was inside. Scattered across the floor were torn boxes and bits of Barbie dolls, Lego, and other toys. Angry that they hadn't found the kind of valuable merchandise they were seeking—things they could return or re-sell for good coin—the thieves destroyed everything just so this woman couldn't repackage her gifts.

The value of the destroyed toys was less than the deductible on her house insurance, yet it was far more than she could afford to replace on her fixed income before Christmas. After I had all the information I needed to complete my report, I sat with her and had a cup of tea. Sometimes policing is just about being present. Those thieves, in their selfish fury, had destroyed an elderly woman's Christmas. And worse, they had stolen her sense of security and comfort in her own home.

A few weeks into the new year, I drove by to see a For Sale sign on her front lawn. After that, I spent every moment I could patrolling the neighbourhoods, hoping I might prevent just one person from going through this by making a show of police presence on the streets.

SHE WAS A CANCER PATIENT, too young to be so sick and weak from the disease and the treatment. She was known to the police, who had to save her more than once from an abusive boyfriend. She had finally secured a no contact order against her abuser, but he was back in her apartment. A friend of the woman had phoned her, learned he was there, and called the police.

When my partner and I arrived, she was pretty out of it, high on painkillers. My partner tried to get some coherent answers out of her while I went into the kitchen with the boyfriend. He explained that he was there to help her, that she'd asked him to come back and take care of her. He claimed the no contact order had been lifted. Our computer check showed that wasn't the case. When he realized he wasn't going to convince me, he got increasingly irate, told me to call in a SWAT team because he wasn't leaving unless he was in a body bag. He opened a drawer and brandished a knife. And then my Smith & Wesson was out of its holster and pointed at his chest.

I was pretty impressed, or at least reassured, by how fast I moved to draw my gun. There was no hesitation, and no doubt in my mind that I'd pull the trigger if he made the slightest move toward me. Another officer might already have fired.

He must have seen how certain I was, because he gave up then.

We arrested him for breaching the no contact order and for threatening to slit the throat of the friend who had called us. There were no charges, though, for threatening an officer of the law—verbal abuse and physical threats were just part of the job.

NO MATTER WHAT MY SHIFT delivered, when I went home I threw myself wholly into the roles of wife and mother. We had endured countless hours of shrieking when Ashley suffered from colic in infancy, but that had passed, and Ashley grew into the easiest little kid you can imagine.

We took her everywhere—even on the drive home from the hospital after she was born, we went to our favourite restaurant for curried chicken. We took her to see her grandparents, to stores and play groups, and to the park—and when she was tired, wherever we were, she just fell asleep. Perhaps it was because both Wayne and I worked shift work and our lives changed daily; getting locked into a routine would have been impossible. We knew parents who had their kids on such a strict schedule and were prisoners to it themselves. The little ones had to be in their own beds at exactly bedtime, rocked a certain way in a certain chair. But there were the Merlos, strolling along the waterfront in the middle of the night with their daughter because it was beautiful out.

Because life was beautiful, and we were just rolling along inside our happy little cocoon.

WORKING GIRLS

5

IN THE FALL OF 1996, I was asked to take part in a hooker sting in Nanaimo. People had been complaining about the activity on a certain stretch in their neighbourhood. Our goal was to catch and punish the johns who exploit prostitutes by paying for their services, though of course we also planned to arrest and charge the prostitutes for engaging in illegal solicitation.

It struck me as an ineffective solution. There's not a little girl alive who dreams of growing up to be a drug-addicted prostitute. A woman with an addiction to street drugs and a dealer who expects to get paid—who threatens, beats, and degrades her like maybe she's been threatened, beaten, and degraded her whole life—isn't going to have a hallelujah moment behind bars and turn her life around just like that. There's such a stigma attached to prostitution that it is almost impossible to escape that life without support, and our society doesn't want to spend the money to offer safe haven and help. That stigma is why sixty prostitutes could disappear off the streets of Vancouver's downtown eastside before anyone took enough notice to figure out that women were dying on Robert Pickton's pig farm. For a long time, nobody looked for them; police services failed to share information. They were, after all, only hookers.

I agreed to take part in the sting with mixed feelings. I was both anxious and curious, but since I'd never done any undercover work, my curiosity won out.

"Feminist" has never been a word I felt applied to me. Although I'd chosen to work in a man's world, at home I embraced a traditionally female role, doing the child care and cooking while Wayne looked after maintenance of the house and the cars. But my female tendencies didn't extend to my wardrobe. I dressed something like a conservative tomboy. I didn't own much feminine clothing, let alone a provocative outfit, so the first thing I had to do was buy "hooker clothes." I managed to find a skimpy shirt and some short spandex pants at a local thrift store, and then I went to buy make-up and hairspray—also items I didn't normally use—but I didn't think of shoes until I got home. The only girly shoes I owned were the white high heels I'd worn on my wedding day. Since I wasn't about to go buy a pair I'd never wear again, I dug them out.

Armed with my costume essentials, I went to work and got done up with the other officers who were tagged to be prostitutes. At least they could help me with my make-up and hair.

I didn't tell Wayne what I was doing. I wasn't sure how he'd react, and I didn't want him to worry. I figured I could tell him later.

The male officers went undercover first to clear the corner. When the prostitutes propositioned them, they were arrested for soliciting and taken to the police station. Then three of us women went to work. Unmarked cars took a position nearby, close enough to intervene if someone tried to pull one of us into a car. There was also an officer in the bushes behind us who was able to listen and react in a second if needed.

We took turns on the corner, the three of us. We'd make the deal with a suspect to exchange sex for money, and direct them to meet us in the back alley—the alley, we'd say, because there are a lot of cops around here. When they drove back there, they were arrested by undercover officers and whisked away. The officer who'd had the conversation with the offender would go sit in one of the undercover cars and write up her arrest notes while the next woman took her turn out on the street.

The key to making a solicitation charge stick is an explicit link between sex and money. Euphemisms like "a full-meal deal" just aren't clear enough for the courts, so we had to draw them out, get the men to state exactly what they wanted to buy. It was definitely outside my comfort zone, wearing make-up and provocative clothing and engaging with strange men in some of the crudest sex talk you can imagine. I think I blushed right through the first, awful conversation, but as the night wore on the role got easier. I got a little creative when I had to, and if the man didn't have enough money, I agreed to lower my prices to get him to go around the back.

Before long, my feet were killing me.

Talking to men who want to hire a prostitute was an eye-opening experience. Some got right to the point and asked how much for this favour, how much for that. Some made small talk like it was a first date and they had to warm up to what they wanted. A few asked if I was a cop. "Do I look like a cop?" I countered, knowing that even if I was standing taller than five-foot-three in those heels, they wouldn't guess a little thing like me was a police officer, so the conversation would continue from there.

The officer behind me in the bushes was a retired minister. Occasionally I'd hear him titter like a schoolgirl. Once in a while, a whisper would come from the dark bushes: "If the nuns in your Catholic girl's school could see you now...." I struggled not to burst out laughing. I was glad he was there, though; I knew he had my back.

It was surprising to me how many men came looking to pick up prostitutes, and how different their reasons were. They ranged from young men wanting a "sure thing" to older men who had just dropped their wives off at the bingo hall nearby and wanted a little social activity while they waited. One man said he was impotent and deeply lonely, and he just wanted to pay someone to talk to him. There was no crime in that, so I sent him away. A young man delivered the worst excuse I heard—he said his grandfather had died that day and he was so upset, he just needed to get his mind off it.

Through the night, I became more and more aware of how many people were affected by prostitution—not just the hookers and the johns but their families, the parents and partners who were soon going to find out about the arrest. Imagine being married to someone for thirty or forty years and then learning they'd been having sex with hookers while you were playing bingo.

Also, there were the neighbours, the people who endured it happening right in front of their homes night after night. Not far from where we hung out on the corner lived a lady who'd grown completely fed up with what she saw going on in front of her house. She'd called the police many, many times. A car would patrol the area and move the prostitutes along, but of course they came right back.

While I was in a car writing up my notes, that woman charged out of her house and made a beeline for the "hooker" on the corner. My undercover colleague, fully aware of how frustrated the residents had become, watched her approach and braced for a confrontation. She was steeling herself when the woman reached into the arm of her sweater and the officer thought she might have a weapon, maybe a knife, up her sleeve.

The woman said, "I know what you're doing out here."

Before the officer could respond, the lady brandished a big Toblerone chocolate bar and handed it to my colleague. "This is for you and your friends to share." Then she turned and went back to her house.

We soon learned the woman had seen us working and had called the station. The dispatcher, familiar with the caller, asked her to describe the prostitutes then confided we were undercover police officers making arrests. The chocolate bar was that woman's way of saying thank you.

As we wrote notes on our evening, we all had a little chocolate to snack on and a few laughs about it.

LIKE PROSTITUTION, ALCOHOLISM IS A serious problem with society-wide repercussions. Police officers see the sad results of alcoholism every day: accidents, assaults, homelessness. Children of alcoholics lose out on parental attention. Often they lack the necessities of life like a safe home, good food, and loving guidance. But I'm convinced nothing can be solved with more arrests, more "tough on crime." What we need is more understanding and more tolerance toward those who are weak, addicted, disadvantaged, and fragile. Kindness won't fix the social problems that plague our cities, of course, but if we're lucky enough to occupy positions designed to help and to protect, we should never misuse those positions to prey on people.

I knew police officers who spent part of their night shifts

picking up DIPPs—the term for people Drunk in a Public Place. Some members engaged in an unofficial competition to snag as many arrests as possible in a shift. An officer's arrest stats mattered.

Hanging around the bars at closing time was like shooting fish in a barrel, and a person who chose to leave the car where it was and walk home often got a surprise. Those looking to bolster their stats could haul in a person who appeared in any way intoxicated—even if that person posed no danger to themselves or anyone else. And anyone detained would have to spend the night sleeping it off in the drunk tank, unable to call anyone (since no charges were laid, the usual rights didn't apply). And maybe they wouldn't make it to work the next morning. Maybe they would lose their job.

Maybe next time, they would decide it was less risky to get off the street and behind the wheel fast, before they were spotted.

It seemed counterproductive to me. It seemed like an abuse of what the law was there to do.

Section 43 of the Liquor Control and Licensing Act—the "drunk in public" legislation—is for the protection of people. It exists to help avoid senseless tragedy, like stumbling out into the road and getting killed. It's supposed to make sure there's a safe place to sober up where there's no risk of being taken advantage of—of being robbed or beaten or raped. The overuse and abuse of Section 43, however, is a violation of human dignity.

One of the worst DIPP arrests I heard about involved a young man recovering from back surgery. He'd gone out with his friends and leaving a downtown bar was approached by a police officer who noticed he was walking funny, maybe stumbling. The young man hadn't been drinking at all—he just hadn't regained the ability to walk normally since his surgery.

But before he could explain about his back surgery, the officer knocked him down and handcuffed his hands behind his back. He was shoved into the back of a police car and made to sleep on a concrete floor for the night. His recovery was compromised; his parents—I knew them, solid people and before this incident, staunch supporters of the RCMP—were livid. Because he was afraid to speak up, they went to the police station and demanded an investigation, but they got nowhere. The complaint was dismissed.

Some officers did more than just compete for the number of arrests. Some held an occasional competition to see who could arrest the prettiest girl. Attractive young women leaving the bar who stumbled on their high heels would find themselves in the back of a patrol car and then in a cell for the night. I heard officers debating whose catch was the finest, whose breasts were the best. They boasted about it. It made my skin crawl though I felt powerless to defend those young women.

In the place where I worked—part of a venerable institution that had built its reputation on honour and accountability—this was how women were viewed: as objects to be inspected, ogled, rated. It may have been only a small number of officers involved, but the system in place made it possible. Those vile competitions reinforced for me just how unequal women were in the eyes of the RCMP.

I always thought my time was better spent patrolling the neighbourhoods. I wanted to prevent cars from being stolen, houses from being robbed, and people from being harmed. And maybe I did, but there's really no way to know. There is no way to measure prevention. Only arrest statistics counted, and my stats for arresting drunks in public were always very low.

There are very few women in the higher ranks of the RCMP, and when a woman does rise, her promotions are met with skepticism. If she's an attractive woman, it's generally assumed that she slept her way to the top. If she's seen as less appealing, hers is considered a token promotion. When I was in uniform, even women were guilty of making those assumptions about other women in the upper ranks. Maybe it's because we knew how women were perceived within the organization, how little respect we were afforded. It was hard for any of us to believe that a woman was promoted based on merit when we knew damn well that women's abilities and intellect were not highly valued or recognized—and when we knew there were a lot of high ranking men who couldn't stand the idea that a woman might outperform them.

In 2012, the RCMP published a gender-based assessment after a study was done to examine whether the promotion and recruitment policies were gender neutral. The report's executive summary emphatically declares that they are neutral, yet the findings also reveal that women are less likely to receive encouragement to enter the Officer Candidate Development Program, the pathway to being appointed a commissioned officer. In fact in 2012, when women accounted for about twenty percent of RCMP members, they still held only about ten percent of the commissioned officers posts, and very, very few had ever cracked the senior management of the organization.

There were over four thousand study respondents, male and female, and they identified two significant concerns that impact the desire to seek promotion. The first is a perceived lack of fairness and transparency in promotional processes; the second is the desire to be promoted based on merit. While fifty-one percent of male non-commissioned officers had applied for two or more positions, only thirty-eight percent of women had.

Some of this may be explained by gender differences (whether nature or nurture). In my experience, most women are not as rank oriented and not as single-minded in their desire to get ahead. And that's not because women aren't leadership material.

Women are ambitious. They do have the desire to lead and to make changes. They just don't want to play by the rules the men have made or compromise their pride or integrity for a promotion. To climb the ladder, they have to battle both the rank structure and the male-dominated hierarchy of the RCMP. For a lot of women, the battle just isn't worth it. When taking a stand at the office gets you labelled a bitch, when refusing to shut up and go along leads your boss to publicly declare that you're obviously suffering from PMS, it gets damn hard to find the strength of conviction to continue.

In my first few years in the RCMP, I'd maintained my silence about a supervisor who had a naked blow-up doll next to his desk and a superior who'd yelled at me to keep my legs shut. But when I overheard female applicants for a newly formed bicycle patrol unit referred to as "ugly, fat-assed female members" in a conversation between another member and our boss, I couldn't keep quiet. Maybe it was easier to confront something that didn't have anything directly to do with me. I went to the superior and complained about the degrading way they'd spoken about women. He just scoffed at me and sent me on my way, though later the junior member he'd had that conversation with came and apologized to me.

Other instances of discrimination were more insidious. Male officers were given permission to take hours-long hockey breaks while on shift. It was deemed important to their fitness. But when another female member and I asked if we could take a one-hour aerobics class on a Tuesday, which would impact two shifts a month, we were told no. Just flat out no.

The RCMP talks about upping its recruitment of women. But no matter how close to equal the female to male ratio gets on the force, until they can acknowledge that a gender-based discrepancy exists, and until they change the fundamental philosophy and structure of the organization, they won't really begin to address gender equity.

It's no surprise to me that the 2012 study also reveals women in the RCMP are more likely than their male counterparts to grow frustrated and leave the organization after twenty years rather than stick it out, hope for improvements, and shoot for a full pension.

When the story of Robert Pickton and Vancouver's downtown eastside prostitutes began to emerge, I thought about the way some of my male co-workers treated female members, and I thought about my time on the street as a hooker. I considered the connecting points. If police officers could feel such animosity toward the women who were their co-workers, trained by and committed to the same organization, then how did those men feel about women who were considered, globally, the lowest of the low? It is reasonable to think some of those women would still be alive if they'd been considered more valuable—valuable enough for someone to pay attention and launch an investigation earlier. It's not about individual officers who are to blame, though. It's systemic. Budget constraints, operational plans, and local municipal priorities always take precedence over what any street cop might deem a priority while rushing from one call to the next.

Still, for me there is an echo between the RCMP management's treatment of women within its ranks and the treatment of sex-trade workers. And the sound that reverberates says, "You are expendable."

I WENT HOME EARLY THE night of the hooker sting. It had been a productive night and we'd made a number of arrests. At about 4 a.m., I was in the shower, washing off all that make-up and hairspray, when Wayne woke up and asked what the hell I was doing home already. I knew I had to come clean, so I sat down on the bed and told him all about my night on the street corner.

To my relief, he was a good sport about it, and he asked with a grin, "Did anybody I know try to pick you up?" And he made me promise that the next time we did a hooker sting, he could come shopping with me to help me pick an outfit.

I kept that promise, but Wayne didn't keep my undercover identity a secret from our friends and family, and for weeks I endured the jokes about my life as a hooker. The fact that I'd worn my wedding shoes was a big hit with everyone.

Ashley was three-and-a-half then. Of course she had no idea what a hooker was, and I had no idea she was paying any attention to the grown-up conversation around her. A few weeks later, I was in the shoe department at Sears with her. She spotted some white high heels and headed over to them. Holding them high, Ashley yelled at the top of her voice, "Mommy, look! These are the shoes you wear when you're a hooker!"

I could feel the caustic stares of other shoppers as their gaze moved from Ashley to me.

We got out of Sears and fled the mall faster than we ever had. Still, for days I worried that someone had followed us, had taken down my plate number and, concerned about the welfare of my child, called Social Services.

It seemed that, despite my best efforts, I wasn't going to be able to keep my work life and my home life truly separate.

Taking a Joke

6

Everyone who works in a field where they come face to face with the tragic and the gruesome on a regular basis knows about black humour. There's an innate human need to put a funny spin on a traumatic incident, to redirect our attention away from something too awful to face directly. I think humour is as much a survival mechanism as the adrenaline rush that puts a body on high alert, or the release of endorphins that mask pain. Maybe black humour is a kind of false bravado, a mask one slips on so no one sees just how shook up you are.

I was not among the responders on the scene when the body of the drowning victim was pulled from the harbour, but I heard about it in great detail. Crabs—great big ones, like the kind we prize for dinner—had eaten their way into the belly of the deceased male. His body, dragged up on to a boat, was moving, squirming with life. While the boat headed to shore, the police officers onboard reached inside the bloated corpse, pulled out the crabs and threw them back into the water so that by the time the body got to the dock, it was stilled.

On shore, there was laughter and some jokes: "I hope I

don't go home to a crab dinner tonight." I know it sounds disrespectful, but all the respect in the world had been shown to the deceased when an officer willingly reached in and pulled out those invaders.

I heard the gory story in a restaurant a few hours later, my co-worker offering up the scene in great detail. I guess we'd hardened ourselves to the gruesome features of our job. We'd built up resilience, learned to put things aside, to bury deep the effects of death and despair. We knew there was always more to come, that a lot of the people we worked alongside every day had seen much more and much worse.

While we ate, my co-worker's voice was booming around the place, and we were laughing at the absurdity of those crabs. Then I noticed people were looking at us. One man, in fact, was striding purposefully toward us.

It was careless, cutting loose like that in public. We knew our antics were out of line, and we got ready for a scolding—got ready to apologize profusely. But the civilian who approached us wasn't looking for an apology. He'd walked over to let us know he'd been complaining too much about his job lately and now he realized he had nothing to complain about at all.

I CAN'T REMEMBER THE FIRST time I saw maggots, but over the years I got used to them. Maggots are actually fly larvae, and flies are proficient parents—they lay their eggs on a ready food source; a human body is as good as any other decaying flesh. But as gross as they are, those tiny, white, wormlike creatures can be useful. For one thing, they follow a predictable pattern of development that offers clues about how long a person has been dead. Plus, they have some medical value.

A colleague I worked with closely went to check on one of the city's street people. He'd suffered a serious cut on his leg that had become infected. Paramedics were also on the scene, and they leaned in to find the gaping wound was full of maggots. My colleague was squeamish, so when a paramedic picked up on her revulsion, he decided to have some fun. He asked her to shine her flashlight on the wound and then laughed at how the beam was moving around as she wavered woozily, trying not to pass out. As the paramedic tweezed the maggots out, he flicked them at her, just to ramp up her disgust. He thought it was hilarious, and in the re-telling, at least, she thought it was funny, too.

Her story fascinated me not because of the paramedic's antics but because that poor man's life was probably saved by those maggots, which fed on the infection and kept it from overwhelming his system. He recovered and was back on the streets in no time.

Other scenes were harder to laugh off. We were called by a man who'd found his brother's body in the bathtub. The victim had suffered from epilepsy, and his brother told us he'd lay in the bathtub when he felt a seizure coming on as a means of preventing injury. It was a smart choice, since he lived alone, but he hadn't survived the last seizure, and he'd lain dead for days in that tub before his brother discovered him.

By then, maggots filled his ears, his eyes, and his mouth.

For me, the visual impact of the scene was never as distressing as the emotional impact. No one should have to see a loved one in that state. The brother was distraught. He had to be kept from the room and answer questions while we dealt with the body. Other family members had to be notified. And the whole time I had to work hard not to wonder too much about what the man in the tub had gone through—whether he'd known he was dying, if he was afraid or sad to be so alone in the end.

IN THE FALL OF 1996, we were dealing with our own sorrows at home. Just days before we were scheduled to take a family trip with Wayne's sister, Jeannie, and her husband, Don, he began to have chest pains. As she raced him to the hospital, Don fell over onto her. It was a massive heart attack, and in emergency, they were unable to revive him. Don was only fifty-one years old, a wonderful man, and all of us were devastated. Just the night before, we'd all had dinner together for the annual celebration of Wayne's birthday and mine, which are close enough to warrant just one cake.

To make things worse, Wayne's father, Jack, was so upset he had a heart attack the evening after Don's death. In need of a quadruple bypass, he was transferred to a hospital in Victoria an hour away, and of course we had to plan and hold Don's memorial service without him. Then the doctors discovered Jack had an abdominal aneurysm and would require surgery on that, too. He was in hospital for months. Jeannie never had time to properly mourn her husband because of the turmoil surrounding her father, and she never really got over the loss of Don, who had been her high-school sweetheart.

For Wayne and I, it was the beginning of a mad juggle to look after everyone.

Getting emotional, showing sensitivity—or worse, fear—is not what you are supposed to do when you're wearing the uniform. The public and your co-workers all count on you to keep it together. You do the best you can to look inscrutable and unafraid. Sometimes, though, the means of distraction you choose don't help your image.

It was almost dusk when another female officer and I arrived in the neighbourhood of Long Lake Heights, where a black bear had been making a nuisance of itself. Some of the houses backed right onto a wooded area, and the bear had taken to paying visits, tearing apart garbage, and generally being a terror. We'd been summoned to assist a conservation officer after a resident called to report the bear was up a tree in the backyard.

The conservation officer took my partner and I to the tree and told us to keep the bear up there while he retrieved and loaded the tranquilizer gun in his truck. His truck was parked about 500 metres away.

"Just keep the bear in the tree. He said it like it was a simple instruction, and maybe in his line of work, it was—but not in ours.

When we asked him how we might go about doing that, he kind of smiled: "I don't care, talk to it, sing to it, dance for it, whatever you have to do."

My partner wasn't confident that would work. "And what do we do if he comes down?"

"Run like a bugger," came the reply.

"If he comes after us, should I shoot him?"

The conservation officer looked at her hip, eyed up her 9 mm and shook his head. "Not with that pea shooter. That'll just piss him off." And then he walked away.

By this time, the whole neighbourhood had caught wind of what was going on, and everybody was out on their back decks watching the action.

About seventy-five feet above us, the bear grunted and growled. He was a full-grown male, and he must have weighed 300 pounds. My partner and I peered up at him, waved branches, yelled up whatever we could think to say. Five minutes, then six, crawled by. The bear climbed up a little further but appeared to slip. Then he looked like he'd decided to come down. We prepared to bolt, but he settled again and stayed where he was. Nine minutes dragged by. Ten. We'd started to sing and dance for the bear. Each minute felt like an hour. Where the hell was that conservation officer? How long could it take to load a tranquilizer gun? He'd been gone for twenty minutes and we were still singing.

It was the performance of a lifetime. It certainly felt that long, anyway.

Finally, the conservation officer returned with his big gun and took up his position. As he aimed, my partner asked, "What if you miss?"

He glanced at her. "I've got more darts in the truck."

So he was going to shoot at this massive, agitated bear and maybe just nick him, maybe just really piss off that big bear, and then this clever conservation officer was going to saunter back to his truck and spend another twenty minutes reloading? Both my partner and I began to giggle, which seemed like the only possible reaction under the circumstances.

The first shot, thank God, hit the bear square in the ass. The officer turned to us and very calmly announced the bear would be down in about five minutes.

"He'll climb down?" I asked.

"No, he'll fall down." In answer to our newfound concerns for the bear's welfare, he assured us that bears fall out of trees every day. "He'll hurt more from the dart in his ass than he will from the fall."

And sure enough, almost exactly five minutes later, that bear fell from the tree and landed at our feet, sound asleep. He was out cold. And he was beautiful.

His paws felt like suede. I know because the three of us each had to grab a limb and pull that three-hundred pound sack of sleeping black bear through the woods. It was getting dark, and rain was beginning to fall. We still had an audience of residents watching as we dragged their neighbourhood nemesis toward the conservation officer's truck. Just as we got to the roadway, my supervisor, Ray Bradford, pulled up. Ray was one of those rare officers who combined an ability to play the game and land a leadership role with ethics, hard work, common sense, and compassion. If they'd had a hundred more like him, the RCMP would have been a very different place.

Ray couldn't contain his grin as he watched us wrestle that

sleeping bear into the cage hitched to the back of truck. While the big bear slumbered, he'd be transported into the wilderness, far enough out that he wouldn't encroach on any homes—or maybe where they wouldn't encroach on him.

By the time we had him safely locked up, we were tired and wet, and Ray thought we should all take a break and get a hot coffee. We were drying out in a diner, laughing, still feeling the euphoria that comes after fear, when my partner asked the conservation officer, "How could it take so fricking long to get to your truck and load that damned tranquilizer gun? We thought you were never coming back."

Without missing a beat, he told us the truth. "Oh, that took about a minute. The rest of the time, the neighbours and I were watching you girls singing to the bear."

THERE ARE BULLIES WHO GET their kicks from demoralizing and humiliating others, and then there are pranksters. Pranks and practical jokes are a way of taking the edge off, of catching someone off guard and having a good laugh with (not at) them. Many of my co-workers used pranks to lighten the mood, to build morale and bolster camaraderie. To blow off a little steam. A prank pokes fun, but it isn't done to make someone look like a fool or feel singled out and devalued.

It's a tricky business, though. Even when the intention is not to hurt feelings or diminish self-worth, the rule of harassment is, ultimately, how the other person feels. I guess the trick is to know your audience.

Wayne still worked for the City of Nanaimo, but he had become a prisoner guard in the cellblock. He was a master of practical jokes at the police station. He filled boots with ice cubes, faked accidents, and even inspired a fiercely strict corporal to get in on the fun and leap out at passersby. Wayne was long overdue to have the tables turned, and I was more than happy to help execute the plan.

Some months before, we'd traded houses with Wayne's parents. They'd been looking to downsize, and we needed a bigger house for our growing family, so swapping was the perfect solution. Our "new" place had a security system, but there were no sensors in the basement where Wayne stored his pride and joy: his Yamaha motorcycle. The Enduro was years old, but it looked like it had just come from the showroom.

Wayne got in the habit of calling me when he worked nights and I was at home just to make sure I'd bolted the basement door. If he thought I sounded dismissive, he'd get more insistent, telling me over and over that I needed to go check until I promised I would and said goodnight. It drove me crazy, his passionate worry, so when someone asked me how they could get Wayne good in return for all the pranks he had pulled on them, I knew exactly what to do. I got the registration information from his motorcycle and gave it to them.

At about 4 a.m. the phone rang. Wayne was distraught. "Janet, they took my bike—you didn't lock the door!" He was shouting into the phone. I assured him I had locked the door, but he knew the bike was gone because he was listening to the chase.

The watch commander had gone down into the cellblock to have coffee with Wayne, and he'd brought along his portable radio, so Wayne couldn't help but hear it all. A few of the members had taken a car far enough out of town that they could blare the sirens without waking anyone. They radioed in that they were in hot pursuit of a blue Yamaha motorcycle. They had asked the dispatcher to run the plate number—the number I had given them—and my husband heard the dispatcher confirm his worst fears: the plate had come back uninsured to Wayne Merlo.

He was wailing into the phone now. "Someone broke into the basement and took my bike.... Can you go check?" I made sure to tell him that we were fine before I laid down the phone and pretended to go downstairs. After a few minutes, I picked the phone back up and confirmed that his bike was gone.

And then I just listened. "I knew it...you didn't lock the fucking door!" And then, "Oh no, he lost control and smashed up my bike.... They're calling the dog out!"

The guys who were in on it laughed about that for a long time, how fast the dispatcher said the dog was being sent out. In real chase situations, the watch commander has the discretion to send the dog after a suspect fleeing on foot. In this instance, dispatching the dog was code for "he fell for it."

I was a little nervous about how mad Wayne might be with me for setting him up, but he wasn't angry at all. No one could say Wayne could dish it out but couldn't take it. He saw my involvement as just a chance to have some fun, not to hurt him. He claimed the prank had aged him ten years, but he was a good sport, and mostly, he was relieved that his precious bike was home safe and sound.

That prank, however, came with a cost. The very next day, Wayne had the alarm company come in and put sensors on the basement door. He even had motion sensors installed. But he probably would have done that eventually anyway, and at least the nightly calls about locking up the basement stopped.

Wayne still has that Yamaha bike, and all these years later, it's still as shiny and new as it was the day he bought it.

THERE'S A DIFFERENCE BETWEEN WHAT'S meant to be funny and what's meant to be degrading, and frankly, most people know the difference.

The Canada Labour Code defines sexual harassment as,

> ...any conduct, comment, gesture or contact of a sexual nature (a) that is likely to cause offence or humiliation to any employee; or (b) that might, on

> reasonable grounds, be perceived by that employee as placing a condition of a sexual nature on employment or on any opportunity for training or promotion.

Training was essential—both for promotion and to keep your skills sharp, to be the best officer possible. And more often than not, training was doled out as a reward. To get some, you had to be on the right side of your supervisor. One morning, I arrived to find in my mail slot a list of "Training Courses Now Available for Women." There were thirty-four of them, and my interest turned to aggravation as soon as I started reading them. Number 9: Communication Skills III, Getting What You Want, Without Nagging. Number 15: Introduction to Parking. Number 23: PMS...Your Problem, Not His.

We had a sergeant in Nanaimo who would have benefitted from getting familiar with that code. His sexual repartee with female officers went far beyond the usual office banter.

One day as I was working in the detachment office, he held up a dildo that had been seized as evidence in a criminal investigation. "Merlo, what the hell happened?" he yelled across the room—a room full of other police officers. "This thing was brand new yesterday. Now it's almost worn out. Did you take it home last night?"

If that had been an isolated incident, it may have been funny. Certainly the onlookers had a good snicker while my face flamed and I tried to concentrate on my paperwork. But there were too many other incidents under the same sergeant.

Once I was assisting him with a very intoxicated, unruly prisoner. The man had arrived at the station in a taxi—the cabbie had dropped him off there after he'd refused to pay the fare. He wasn't happy about that. It took two of us to get him subdued and down to the cellblock, and in the scuffle, the sergeant cut his thumb on the handcuffs. While the guard went to get a

Band-Aid, the sergeant held up his wounded, meaty hand with its hairy knuckles and asked me to kiss it better. I grimaced and shook my head thinking, "Here we go again." Just as the guard came back in with the Band-Aid, the sergeant shoved that hand in his pants pocket and said that, on second thought, that's where it was when it got hurt. He suggested I kiss the thumb and everything else down there better, too. His pants were always too tight, straining against his blocky frame, and when he wriggled his fingers inside his pocket it looked particularly gross. I remember the guard's face registered shock and revulsion and probably mirrored my own.

I called the sergeant a pig that time—I couldn't bite off the words fast enough—and I whirled around and got the hell out of the cellblock. Then I went on with my duties. There was no option to confide with someone or to take a little time to decompress. I just had to carry around my lingering nausea and try not to let my anger and disgust spill over into my work with the public.

Those insulting incidents were like the maggots eating me up inside. I found a way to deal with the grotesque and the tragic, but the belittling personal attacks were not so easily brushed off. Some people seem immune to bullying and harassment, and perhaps the things that hurt me so deeply would have meant nothing to someone else. People deal with things differently, but when co-workers criticized and demoralized each other, when they were brusque with the public or even openly nasty, I sometimes wondered if that wasn't their way of coping, if they turned all the grief and frustration that were a part of our daily jobs back on others in cruel ways.

I never considered turning my distress against someone else, never wanted to hurt another person because I was hurting. Instead, I internalized it all, and slowly, I turned it against myself.

No One To Tell

A man shot himself on a quiet logging road leading up to a mountain. The passerby who found the victim and called it in had driven past him just minutes before, had seen him standing by his car. The caller drove up the mountain, turned around, and came back to find the man dead in the middle of the road. A shotgun was lying with him.

The coroner was summoned, and once we determined the man had died from a self-inflicted wound, we had to wonder if he'd come alone or if there was someone else—someone the man had hurt or killed before taking his life. We couldn't see anyone, but to be sure, we had the police dog search the surrounding area. Nothing was found.

After finishing the investigation, the coroner's office called the local funeral service that held the contract to collect such bodies. Don, one of the regulars with that service, showed up. Don and I had been together on a few scenes like this over the years.

It was late afternoon by this time, and we wanted to get things cleaned up before the sun went down on that dark road. The shotgun blast had blown off half the man's face and head. After we placed his remains in a body bag, Don and I worked our way up the road, picking pieces of skull and brain tissue up out of the gravel.

The next time I saw Don was months later at the hospital where he also worked as a porter. I was pregnant with my second baby and in a lot of pain that wasn't, as it turned out, labour. It was Don who wheeled me down to have an ultrasound. He stuck around to see if I was okay. While the young technician moved the wand across my distended belly and punched information into her system, Don asked me if I'd been back on the mountain lately. The technician smiled and asked if we went skiing together.

Don winked at me and said, "No—Janet and I do other things up on the mountain together."

Then he left, and left the technician floundering, looking from Don to my very pregnant belly, trying to discern what he might have meant.

I couldn't tell her what we did up on that mountain, couldn't ever find words to describe how a life ends in fragments cast out onto a dusty road. Those weren't the sort of things any of us discussed. Don's inexplicable comment was as close as we would ever come to talking about that suicide or any of the other awful things we witnessed. Yet seeing Don in the hospital stirred up my memories of the scene on the mountain, and it was so clear, it was like living it all over again.

The ultrasound diagnosed kidney stones, and while I endured the passing of those, my mind turned the scene over, left me wondering why someone would put a gun to his head. Was it because that man felt there was nobody in the world he could turn to, nobody he could fall apart in front of and trust that they would help put him together again?

There was never an opening to talk about it with anyone. You couldn't discuss it at the dinner table. You didn't want to burden your family. You certainly couldn't describe that terrible scene and how you felt about it over coffee with the other moms while your children played nearby. And raising your feelings at work would only lead others to question your professionalism, even if you never shied away from attending the next call when it came, no matter how shook up you were about the last.

So we never spoke of the lingering images we carried or the humiliations we suffered. It would have been like admitting weakness. And bullies can smell weakness; they thrive on it. We kept our mouths shut, and we allowed the horrible things we'd experienced to take root inside us, just as we allowed the rot within our organization to proceed unchecked.

It was only years later that I learned so many others suffered the same way I did.

Honest Answers

7

Despite the nasty reaction to my first pregnancy, Wayne and I were anxious to have another child, so I was delighted to be expecting. Five years had passed since my first, and this time around there were no curses or vulgar comments and far fewer grumblings. I did sense antipathy coming from some of my co-workers, but I tried to take it in stride—I'd been prepared for much worse.

In March of 1998, our second daughter, Erin, was born. She was fairer and quieter than her bubbly sister, more reserved and shy—more like her mother. Her arrival brought tremendous joy back into our family, which had been hit so hard by Don's death and Jack's medical struggles.

After a six-month maternity leave, I returned to work. Ashley was just beginning school, and Erin, thank goodness, was as adaptable to a changing schedule as her sister had always been. When I was off work, I would strap her into the Snugli and take her out. Often, I'd take her to the bingo hall to visit her grandmother, and all the ladies would reach out to stroke the little arms and legs that waved and kicked out in front of me.

There's a lot of heartbreak in police work, and when you have your own children at home—when you're under the thrall of such overwhelming love and fierce devotion to their protection—it is hard to keep those emotions from spilling over whenever any child is harmed.

For me, the hardest thing was trying not to bring it all home.

I went to a domestic assault where it was alleged the male had thrown an eight-month-old baby across the room at her mother. The baby was fine, but the parents were both arrested; Children and Families were called to place the baby in foster care. Waiting for the on-call social worker that night, the 9-1-1 operators and the dispatchers passed around and cooed at the baby while I went home and retrieved supplies, some diapers and clothes, so the baby could be changed. Of course I peeked in at my own baby girl, sleeping safe and sound, and I thought how different these little girls' lives would be.

ERIN WAS STILL AN INFANT when a woman showed up at the detachment office with her seven-year-old daughter. The little girl had gone up to the neighbour's that afternoon and had come home with a chilling story about a sexual assault she'd just experienced. The girl needed to be examined, so we advised the mother to take her straight to the hospital while my partner and I went to pick up the suspect. I noticed a camera on his nightstand, and one little girl's sock near the sliding glass door, but we were only authorized to take in the suspect and hold him pending investigation.

At the hospital, I went into the examination room with the doctor and the young girl. Although a curtain was pulled between us so I was out of sight, I could hear his questions and

CONSTABLE JANET MERLO'S BADGE—mounted, encased in acrylic, and received upon her retirement from the RCMP in 2010.

TRAINING COURSES NOW AVAILABLE FOR WOMEN

1. Silence, the Final Frontier: Where No Woman Has Gone Before.
2. The Undiscovered Side of Banking: Making Deposits.
3. Combating the Imelda Marcos Syndrome: You Do Not Need New Shoes Everyday.
4. Parties: Going Without New Outfits.
5. Man Management: Discover How Minor Household Chores Can Wait Until After the Game.
6. Bathroom Etiquette I: Men Need Space in the Bathroom Cabinet Too.
7. Bathroom Etiquette II: His Razor Is His.
8. Valuation: Just Because It's Not Important to You . . .
9. Communication Skills I: Tears-The Last Resort, Not the First.
10. Communication Skills II: Thinking Before Speaking.
11. Communication Skills III: Getting What You Want, Without Nagging.
12. Driving a Car Safely: A Skill You CAN Acquire.
13. Party Etiquette: Drinking Your Fair Share
14. Telephone Skills: How to Stop Talking and Hang Up
15. Introduction to Parking
16. Advanced Parking: Reversing Into A Space.
17. Overcoming Anal Retentive Behavior: Leaving the Towels on the Floor.
18. Water retention: Fact or Fat.
19. Cooking I: Bringing Back Bacon, Eggs and Butter.
20. Cooking II: Bran and Tofu are Not For Human Consumption.
21. Cooking III: How Not to Inflict Your Diets on Other People.
22. Compliments: Accepting Them Gracefully.
23. PMS: Your Problem . . . Not His.
24. Dancing: Why Men Don't Like To.
25. Sex-It's For Married Couples Too.
26. Classic Clothing: Wearing Outfits You Already Have.
27. Household Dust: A Harmless Natural Occurrence Only Women Notice.
28. Integrating Your Laundry: Washing It All Together.
29. Ballet: For Women Only.
30. Oil and Gas: Your Car Needs Both.
31. Learning to Go in Public Restrooms.
32. Appreciating the Humor of the Three Stooges.
33. "Do These Jeans Make My Butt Look Big?" - Why Men Lie.
34. TV Remotes: For Men Only.

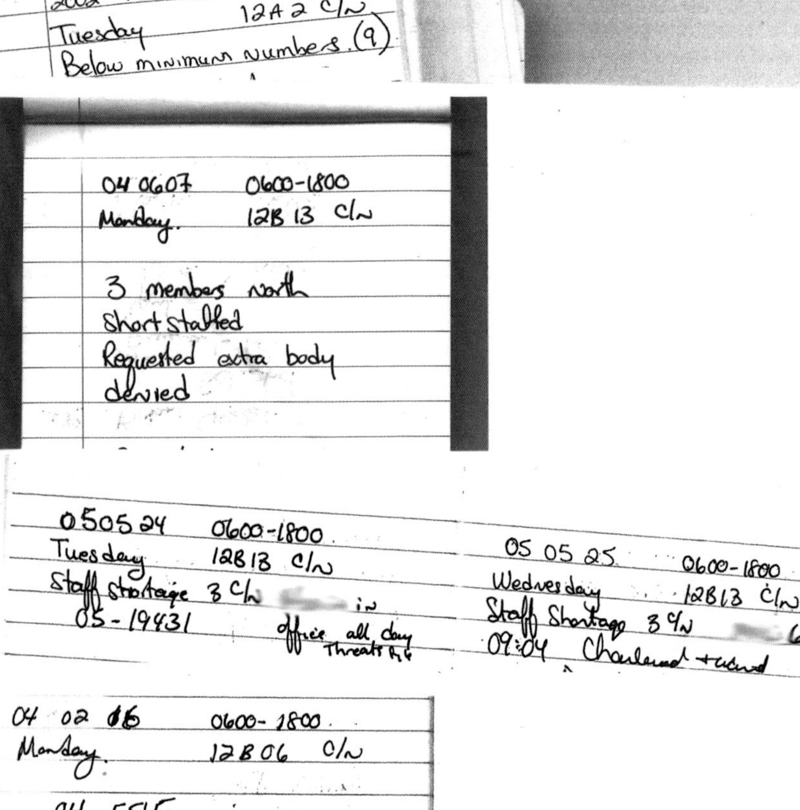

2002 10 15 0700-1900
Tuesday 12A 2 C/W
Below minimum numbers. (9)

04 06 07 0600-1800
Monday. 12B 13 C/W

3 members north
Short staffed
Requested extra body
denied

05 05 24 0600-1800
Tuesday 12B13 C/W
Staff shortage 3 C/W [illegible] in
05-19431 office all day
Threats [illegible]

05 05 25 0600-1800
Wednesday 12B13 C/W
Staff Shortage 3 C/W [illegible] 63
09:04 [illegible]

04 02 06 0600-1800
Monday. 12B06 C/W

04-5515

351 ABP

10' Kenwood Speaker
phoenix Gold Amp

5517.

5522
11:45 Am
3 members working 2 zones today.
Message sent to W/C asking for extra bodies but was ignored.

No help assigned. numerous files given to 12B06 (12B13) and Cst [illegible] in 12B09.
Jim

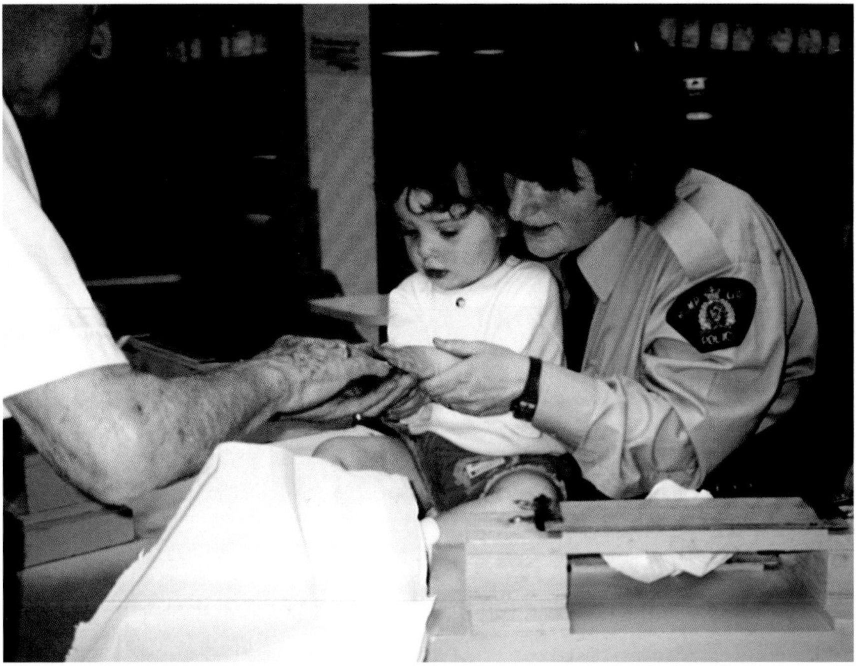

(TOP) CONSTABLE MERLO FINGERPRINTING HER daughter Ashley for Child Find during the 1993-94 school year.

(BOTTOM) MERLO KAYAKING AT KILMORY Resort in Swift Current, Newfoundland and Labrador

Minister of Public Safety — Ministre de la Sécurité publique

OCT 1 2 2007

Constable Janet Merlo

Dear Constable Merlo:

Thank you for writing to express your support for the appointment of Mr. William J.S. Elliott as the new Commissioner of the Royal Canadian Mounted Police (RCMP) and your concerns about the RCMP transfer policy.

First, please accept my apology for the extended length of time it has taken for a reply to your concern, which you sent some months ago. A combination of factors including the need of my officials to explore fully the matter you raised, along with the requirement to assess the response in the light of similar and sometimes competing factors, added to the sheer volume of requests which come to me, has created a delay which is not appropriate. I am pleased I can finally respond.

Canada's New Government is committed to ensuring that the RCMP is an effective and accountable national police force. Our government is taking action. Through the appointment of a new commissioner and the establishment of a Task Force to review the governance and management practices of the Force, we are demonstrating our resolve to ensure the accountability of the RCMP.

The appointment of Mr. Elliott as Commissioner will provide strong leadership to bring about the changes needed to make the RCMP a better and stronger organization for the 26,000 men and women who serve this country from coast to coast.

Please be assured that a copy of your correspondence will be forwarded to Mr. Elliott for his consideration regarding the RCMP transfer policy.

Thank you for sharing your views on this important issue.

Yours sincerely,

Stockwell Day, P.C., M.P.
Minister of Public Safety

c.c.: Mr. William Elliott
Commissioner of the Royal Canadian Mounted Police

IN 2007, CONSTABLE MERLO wrote to RCMP Commissioner William Elliott to identify existing problems in the RCMP's transfer policies and to raise concerns regarding sexual harassment within the force. The response came in the form of this letter from the Minister of Public Safety, Stockwell Day.

Royal Canadian Mounted Police

Gendarmerie royale du Canada

Deputy Commissioner
Chief Human Resources Officer

Sous-commissaire
Dirigeant principal des Ressources humaines

October 2nd, 2009

Dear Cst. Merlo:

Thank you for your correspondence of August 19th, 2007. I am responding to you on behalf of the Commissioner.

Your correspondence indicates concerns with the application of the compassionate transfer policy and allegations of harassment. As you are aware, the RCMP does not take these allegations lightly and in fact has an obligation to provide a harassment free environment for all of our employees.

It is my understanding that an investigation has been initiated and a review is underway in the Pacific Region. I have forwarded your letter to the Pacific Region Human Resources Officer. Your concerns will be reviewed and someone from that office will contact you in due course.

Yours sincerely,

Deputy Commissioner Peter D. Martin
Chief Human Resources Officer

c.c.: Human Resources Officer, Pacific Region
Commissioner William J.S. Elliott

Received Nov 1, 2009

A FULL TWO YEARS after her initial letter to Commissioner William Elliot, expressing concerns about the RCMP's compassionate transfer policy and sexual harassment within the force, Merlo received this letter from Deputy Commissioner Peter Martin.

Royal Canadian
Mounted Police

Human Resources Branch
Pacific Region

Gendarmerie royale
du Canada

Ressources humaines
Région du Pacifique

Human Resources Officer
Pacific Region
5255 Heather Street
Vancouver, BC V5Z 1K6

December 5, 2011

Re: Your Client

Dear

This letter is to confirm that Constable Janet Merlo, Regimental Number 43401, retired from the Royal Canadian Mounted Police on March 25, 2010.

At no time did Constable Merlo enter into any financial agreements or receive any settlements from the RCMP.

I can also confirm that there no ongoing negotiations between Constable Merlo and the RCMP.

Yours truly,

A LETTER SENT TO Merlo's husband from the Human Resources Office of the RCMP to dispel a rumour within the Nanaimo detachment that Constable Merlo had received a financial settlement from the RCMP upon retirement.

her responses. His exam concluded there was no vaginal trauma, but there was trauma extending about three inches into her anus, tears on both sides. The doctor asked her how her bum had been hurt, but she said she couldn't talk about it.

While I listened, the doctor asked: "Did this happen today?"

"Yes."

Doctor: "Do you know of anything that may have made your bum sore?"

"I'm not sure."

"Did your bum get sore today?"

"Yes." Her voice was calm but diffident.

"Can you remember what made it sore?"

"I can't remember."

Interviewing children is a very special skill. Sometimes they're reluctant, whether shy or afraid, or they don't understand the question. If you ask something they don't understand, their imagination can kick in and skew the responses. And with young children, you only have a brief window, maybe fifteen minutes, to gather your information before they lose interest or before they sense that people are agitated, and then they start saying what they think you want to hear so they can get out of the interview.

Questions that ask for simply yes or no are complicated for another reason—children are small and they have no power, so most are very good at pleasing. They generally want to say yes. They aren't trying to lie—it's just that they want to get along, which is always preferable to getting in trouble.

The doctor asked if her bum got sore when she went to the neighbour's house, and she said yes. After a few more questions, she offered that the neighbour had kissed it. The doctor asked: "Did he touch your bum with anything?"

"I can't remember.... No."

"Did some part of his body hurt your body?"

The little girl initially hesitated, but then said yes.

I drew a rough picture of a person on a piece of paper and handed it to her with a pen. I asked if she could circle the part of his body that had hurt her. She circled the hand.

The doctor took over again. "His hand hurt your bum?"

"Yes, when he stuck his finger in my bum hole."

"Did anything else go into your bum hole?"

"No."

Children are so precise in their answers. If you ask a question that just requires yes or no, that's all the answer you'll get. It's far more productive to ask questions that will trigger an explanation or some description.

My partner was back at the office, filling in the paperwork for a search warrant of the suspect's residence. We wanted to include the camera in the warrant, but we'd need to know the suspect had used it. I asked the little girl if he had taken any pictures. She shook her head and said no, so I relayed that back to my partner. As the medical examination continued, however, the little girl looked over at me and simply volunteered, "He couldn't take a picture because the batteries were dead."

Aha. I had asked a closed yes or no question, and she had answered truthfully but not completely. Children think very differently than adults, and as an investigator, you have to know that. It's so easy to blow an interview with a child. Asking if he took pictures is completely different than asking if he tried to take pictures. Fortunately, there was still time to put the camera in the warrant—who knew what might be on that roll of film.

In the end, that articulate little girl provided a great statement. It included how she'd lied to her assailant, telling him that if he let her go home for dinner, she would keep their secret. As soon as she got home, she told her mom what had happened.

We got the search warrant we needed that night, and recovered her socks from beside and under his bed. The case went to court and led to a conviction.

A TEAM OF US WERE executing a warrant for the arrest of a man whose grown daughter had accused him of sexual assault and other brutal violence. I was deeply involved in the case. I'd interviewed the woman many times, and I had seen her injuries. You can pretend to be hardened in a professional way, but the savagery of what had been done to her had shaken me up. Now we were in position to make an arrest in the case, but it was complicated. We had reason to believe the man had guns in his house, so a strategic plan was in place. I was waiting for coordinating instructions, for the plainclothes officers who were supposed to approach the front door first, when I got a message over the radio to call the sergeant's cellphone.

"Tony's pizza," he answered. "What kind of pizza do you want?"

Startled, I shot back, "Pepperoni." I figured playing along would get us past the nonsense and to the reason for the call faster. The sergeant knew my involvement in this case—he had signed off over many months on my interviews with the complainant—and he knew that waiting in a situation like this caused a weird mix of boredom and anxiety. But his next comment suggested he didn't really care about what the officers on his watch were up to.

"I don't have any pepperoni," he said to me, "but I got a big Italian sausage I'd love to give you."

I was sitting alone in my car, waiting to arrest a man I had every reason to believe was a heinous sexual offender and this—a joke about a sausage—was what my boss wanted to tell me. The shudder went right through to my bones. It was as if he had no filter at all, as if no situation could temper his obscene mouth.

I HAD NO PATIENCE FOR parents who pointed at me and warned their children to be good or else I'd take them to jail.

The last thing I wanted was for a child to fear me or any police officer. Fear leads to silence and to secrets.

At the mall one afternoon, a little boy recognized me and warned my daughter that she'd better be good or I would "shoot her dead." My own child was unimpressed. Neither of my girls knew much about what their parents did for a living when they were small, and we wanted to keep it that way for as long as possible, so we didn't talk much about work in their presence.

I always thought it was important for children to trust the police, to have faith that we'd help if they needed it. The most effective way to instill that trust, and to foster smart choices in children, is to engage in public education. I loved attending schools, talking to the students about my role in the community.

But even that was not without risks. I'd been shushed by five-year-old children who were trying to have their own conversation in class, and I'd been asked over and over again how many people I had shot. The answer—none—was always a big disappointment for some of the kids. I'd also been brought up short while delivering a pedestrian safety session to an elementary school class. I'd shown the video and handed out the colouring sheet to drive home the safety rules, but while I was recapping, a young girl raised a point about hypocrisy.

"If you want us to go to a crosswalk, why did a policeman jump out of the woods into the street in front of Mommy's car the other day? That wasn't safe!"

I knew just who she meant, too. There was a traffic member who loved giving tickets and was known for suddenly popping out of the bushes with a radar gun and standing in the road to stop an offending vehicle. Hardly a demonstration for roadway safety.

Sometimes, I went to my own girls' schools. On literacy night, I donned my uniform to read storybooks. Other times, I would stop in just to say hi to the kids in the hallways so they would remember that police officers were normal people in their community. They knew me as "Erin's mom" or "Ashley's mom," and that was my favourite way of being addressed.

But some kids recognized me for another reason. I'd visited their homes on official business. Our eyes would meet, even briefly, and I would see the anxiety in their faces, the fear I was going to say or do something and their peers would know that I'd been to their house, that something bad was going on there. They were afraid I would blow their cover, embarrass them. But I never let on. For their sake and mine, I kept a wall between the part of me that was a police officer and the part of me that was somebody's mom.

I HATED SEEING FEAR IN a child's eyes when a parent was out of control, drunk or enraged or both, and I hated the tears that came when they watched a parent being taken away by the police. I always took time to reassure them that even though grownups sometimes made bad decisions, the child was still loved. The words might sound hollow, but I'd remind myself that hope was worth holding onto, that people could change, that sometimes good things came after intervention.

I went to a townhouse one morning after a father woke to find his toddler, a boy not even two years old, missing. The stroller was gone, too. The dad admitted he'd gone next door the night before to play cards, leaving the boy sleeping and the door unlocked. When he came home, he went straight to bed without checking on the little boy. Again, he'd left the door unlocked, so he didn't know if the boy had disappeared while he was out or while he was asleep, but he was pretty sure it was the boy's mother who'd taken him. She had a severe mental illness and was not allowed unsupervised access to her child.

Another officer and I went to the rooming house where she lived. Sure enough, the stroller was parked outside. When the woman refused to open her door, we forced our way in. We found the boy unharmed and took the mother, who was off her medication, to the hospital for assessment. Of course we had to report the whole incident to the Ministry of Children and Families. The father was counselled on his poor judgement and was receptive to taking responsibility for his mistakes and not repeating them. He went on to do a great job of raising his son as a single parent. I often saw them walking hand in hand, father and son, along the waterfront.

Wayne's parents had an old motor home, and in the summer they would drive up to a First Nations reserve at the north end of the city and park for weeks on the waterfront. It was nearby but such a world apart. At low tide, the campers would dig for clams, and at night, fires dotted the beach.

When Kay and Jack took a break from the beach and went home for a few days, they'd leave the motor home there so we could go up and camp in that beautiful spot. But after the girls came along, Wayne lost all interest in going camping with us, so I would take the girls and go up for a night or two while he stayed home alone.

I don't know why that happened, and I didn't know the right questions to ask to understand it. But that was the beginning of the girls and I doing things without him.

So much of policing is about relationships. I had an ongoing relationship with a foster family who frequently took in children in need. Often those kids had been through so much turmoil, and their behaviour reflected it. The woman called me about a boy in her care and asked if I'd drop by on an unofficial visit and give them some advice. She'd caught the twelve-year-old boy trying to access child pornography on the Internet and wanted me to explain to him how serious it was—how much trouble it could cause for his foster parents if their computer ever came into question. How they could even lose the privilege of offering a safe home to kids like him.

When I finished, the boy said he understood, and then he began to cry. He said he'd never do it again—he didn't mean to get her in any trouble. I thought we were done, but he put his head down and said, "I was just looking to see if I could find myself on there."

His foster mother and I looked at each other.

It all came tumbling out of him then, the depth of the sexual abuse he had suffered at the hands of his parents. He'd been humiliated and hurt, raped by grown men while his father videotaped the assaults. The boy didn't know if his dad ever put any of it up on those websites, but he was scared that if it was there, some of his school friends might be trolling those sites, come across it, and recognize him being sexually assaulted.

That night was the first time he ever disclosed the extent of the abuse he'd endured, and it went a long way in explaining his behavioral issues.

Sometimes, people mistakenly believe that talking about trauma is an instant fix, that it's like lancing a boil and letting the poison out—you heal up fast after that. But when the poison has built up for a long time it goes right through you, everywhere, and recovery takes a lot of treatment and a lot of time.

Still, identifying the problem is the crucial first step. I knew two boys, brothers, who'd been abused and were in foster care. Every day, they ran away. At first, we were called in to look for them, but on the days the police didn't locate them, they returned home at dusk. Every day: gone and then home at nightfall. Nobody understood it until one of them spilled: the abuse they suffered at the hands of their parents happened at night, in the dark. Fury and harm woke them up out of deep sleeps, no lights on. They were both terrified of the dark.

For the boy who was looking for himself on the porn sites, the secret had been crashing around inside him and coming out in all kinds of inappropriate ways. Telling it made it possible for him to access the right kind of help. Gradually, he healed, and through the years I saw him grow into an amazing young man.

WHEN ERIN WAS ABOUT THREE and Ashley eight, Wayne and I volunteered our daughters to take part in the production of a training video that would help police officers learn how to interview children. We couldn't let them know they were part of a process or it would taint their answers.

The plan was simple and safe. I was to show the girls a ten-minute video of a cartoon before bringing them into the police station, where they would be questioned about the video they had seen—every parent knows that kids love to describe what they've watched in great detail—and the interview would be taped. Since the girls were five years apart, the results would show how age and development makes a difference to the way they respond to questions.

I got them to sit and watch the video, so I'd done my part.

At the police station, they went upstairs to the interview room, and I hung around the office. After a little while, the female member doing the interview paged me. She asked if the girls had watched the cartoon that morning. I assured her they had, and she assured me they had both denied watching a cartoon.

I thought that was really odd.

A few minutes later, she paged me a second time. She'd asked about the cartoon again, and again they had said no, they didn't know about the cartoon. I was baffled. What was wrong with my children?

And then it hit me. I called her back. "They don't call it a cartoon. Ask them if they watched a video this morning."

That was exactly the problem. Using the wrong word, an unfamiliar word, had changed the entire outcome of the interview. If instead the interviewer had asked a broader, more open-ended question—"Can you tell me what you did at home this morning?"—she likely would have heard about the video much sooner, and then she could have asked a follow-up question.

The officer who made that training video and I often laughed about it. Ashley and Erin had done a little training of their own with her, but they had thrown a surprise my way, too. When the member was trying to break the ice with them, she'd asked Erin some basic questions about me—what my name was, that sort of thing. When she'd asked, "Does your mommy work?" Erin had responded "No."

Perplexed, my co-worker had pursued it. "So what does Mommy do?"

"She knits."

"Does she also work?"

"Nope, she just knits."

I was gone from the house for forty-eight hours every week, yet my own daughter didn't know I had a job. She knew Daddy went to work, but God knows where she thought Mommy went. I guess I was doing a very good job of keeping my life compartmentalized.

Working Long

8

Every week, constables worked two day shifts that ran from seven in the morning until seven at night. Following a swing day, we worked two twelve-hour nightshifts. We'd get four days off in between, so our lives rotated on that eight-day cycle. Some shifts were crazier than others, but they all had their challenges. A day shift in the early years of the new millennium could unfold something like this.

It's 6:30 a.m. when I get to work. We have to arrive about thirty minutes before our shifts start so we have time to get into uniform and gather all the equipment an officer might need—rain jacket, Kevlar gloves, hat, disposable gloves. I load my gun and chamber a round to make sure it's ready to fire if I need it. That's just one of the routines, the checks and double checks that officers do every day to ensure the safety of both the members and the public. After that, I head to the main office to sign out a portable radio and a Taser, because I've been trained to use one—training that included linking arms with colleagues and having the voltage course through us, cinching our muscles tight, until one officer found the strength to break the chain.

At 6:45, I join my watch mates, the entire oncoming shift, in the staff lunch room for the morning briefing. I pay close attention because I like to know who else is working from the other sections—traffic, drugs, property crime—and what I need to keep in mind during the shift.

Attendance is taken. RCMP regulations stipulate the minimum number of police officers who should be on the job at any given time. In the area for which our detachment is responsible, the minimum number of officers for this shift is nine, but there are just seven of us here today. Protocol dictates the watch commander on duty call somebody in on overtime. It's an issue of officer safety as well as public safety.

I start thinking about what ifs. What if there's a multi-car wreck with fatalities out on the highway? What if there's a hostage taking or a shooting rampage at a school? If anything like that happens, we'll need those extra members in a hell of a hurry. I keep my mouth shut and look around hopefully. Sometimes, one of the males speaks up, requests more bodies out there, and gets a positive response—or at least a less negative response than the response I might engender.

No one else says anything, so I take a deep breath, raise the issue of manpower shortage, and ask about calling in more officers.

Maybe I don't say it sweetly enough because the watch commander laughs acerbically. "Boys, Merlo's on the rag again."

Not all of my co-workers laugh, but nobody backs me up, either. Nobody says "Come on, we really could use more members out there."

The watch commander repeats his promise to call somebody in on overtime if something big enough happens, and reads the "pass on"—the stuff we need to know such as what happened overnight and what's happening today. Stolen cars, road closures, that sort of thing. While we're briefing, the night shift is coming off the road, and calls are still coming in, so things are getting backed up. This morning, nothing's urgent enough for one of us to have to leave the briefing.

Before I head out, I have to complete the same routine we all do every morning. First, I get my kit bag. It's full of everything I might need in the course of a long shift, including my personal flashlight, my digital recorder, ticket books, court notices, and snacks. You have to make sure you have all the necessities before you leave the office because if it gets busy out there, you may not have the opportunity to get back.

At least now that we have computers in the car, we don't have to lug our big accordion file folder and all our paperwork along for the ride. It isn't unusual to have about twenty SUI, or Still Under Investigation, cases. Domestic assaults, sexual assaults, internal thefts, arson. Any case that falls under the criminal code and still needs some follow-up—like a statement taken or court documents completed—is SUI. So we take all our files with us, on paper or online, when we head out, just in case there's a lull and we have time to work on them during the day.

On television and in the movies, cops just climb into their cars and tear off. Before I can get behind the wheel of the RCMP car I've been assigned, however, there's a complex routine I have to complete, and all of it has to be documented in my notebook. First, I do a vehicle inspection. I look for any new damage, check the headlights, brake lights, and turn signal lights. You can hardly pull somebody over and issue them a ticket for a light that's out on their car if you have one out yourself. I check the emergency lights and the siren, too, because the worst time to find out they aren't working is when a priority call comes in.

I make sure the trunk contains all the emergency equipment it's supposed to: flares and pylons for accident scenes, a reflective vest, a fire extinguisher, and a first-aid kit. There's a long list, and the car can't leave the compound until you've made sure you have the correct amount of each item, that things didn't get depleted during the last shift.

Once I know the trunk is okay, I turn my attention to the back seat. I have to search it, too, and document anything I find. The last person in the back seat may have ditched some evidence related to a crime down behind the seat. They might have stashed drugs or a knife, and you must ensure it's safe to put somebody else back there. You don't want to be responsible for someone in your car getting poked with a dirty syringe. Of course the car is searched each time a person gets in and out—it's the only way to know who, exactly, stashed what. At the end of the shift, a search is also mandatory, but you can't be sure the member who drove this car on the previous shift didn't forget or miss something.

I've been at the office for an hour. Finally, I can shift into gear and begin the real work of my day.

Just before I leave, I have a few words with my zone partner. Nanaimo, a rapidly growing city since the 1990s, is broken into three zones: south, central, and north. We usually work central, and my partner is a great guy who I've worked with for years. We head off in different cars, different directions, but promise to connect up later.

I let the dispatcher know that I'm on patrol. By this time, there's usually a few calls backed up. The easiest calls are over before they've begun. A woman has complained that her car's been stolen. Before I even arrive, she's called dispatch back, embarrassed, to say she found the car—she'd just forgotten where she'd parked it. The acronym for this kind of call is NFARCH: No Further Action Required; Concluded Here.

But imagine now that things start to get more complicated. Maybe there's been a rash of calls from people who all went out in the morning to find their cars had been broken into overnight, a string of cars from one end to the other. I have to talk to all fourteen of them, document information on each owner and each vehicle. I have to note what each complainant says is missing and find out if there are serial numbers for any of it. I have to note, too, the specifics of all the damage for the insurance companies, and if it seems like there may be fingerprints, I have to call out the Forensic Identification section to dust for them. This could take the whole morning, but not quite two hours in, I get called away to an accident.

Let's say it's an accident involving three vehicles. A serious accident with serious injuries. There are ambulances on scene when I arrive, and I assist with moving the victims while I'm trying to learn their identities and their roles in the accident. The fire department is working, too. They've made sure nothing's about to catch fire, and they're extracting someone from the car that sustained the most damage. Other officers have put up pylons and are managing traffic control, keeping everyone moving safely, or as safely as possible, given that every driver is looking out their side window to see what's happened instead of watching where they're going. We're all hoping one of these "lookie loos" doesn't cause a second accident because we've got enough to contend with here.

At least all the drivers are accounted for, and at least none of the vehicles involved were stolen, so we don't have to call in a dog to try and chase a driver who's fled the scene.

But there is a fatality at the scene, a dead passenger in that crumpled car, so I notify the coroner's office, and we call in the special traffic section to do the meticulous investigation that happens at a fatal crash. The body has to remain where it is until they get here. The ambulances race off with their injured passengers while we close off the road.

I call tow trucks and notify the city that the roadway needs to be treated for a gasoline spill. Once the specialized section arrives and takes over that scene, I'm free to move on. But moving on means locating and notifying the deceased's next of kin, either in person if they're local or by contacting the detachment where they live to deliver the terrible news.

So in the middle of a hectic day, an RCMP officer might find herself standing in someone's living room telling them their spouse has met a tragic end. And no matter how emotional, how heartbreaking, how hard you have to work not to put yourself in those shoes, you must stay calm. You have to keep it together, be the embodiment of understanding and strength in the face of a family member who is distraught. That's not an easy thing to do, and it's even harder if you've recently experienced a loss of your own and the feelings are still raw.

You don't ever get used to it, though you get better at steeling yourself. Because you have to get back on the road.

So often, a work shift requires shifting from the banal to the tragic to the weird. My next call might be a disturbance at an apartment building, where a man claims another tenant has gone crazy and is making a ruckus in the hallways and the stairwell. The caller meets me at the front door of the building and says the man has calmed down and gone into his apartment. I ask specifically what he was doing. Cursing, for one thing, the complainant tells me. "And he was bustin' his carrots."

I'm not familiar with that turn of phrase, so I ask for a clearer explanation but again I get, "He was bustin' his carrots." I chuckle a little and say I've heard a lot of sayings in my career, but I really don't understand this one. The man looks at me, and it's obvious he's getting frustrated by how dense I am. "What are you, fucking blind?" He points to the ground at the edge of the sloped parking lot, and that's when I see them: dozens of broken carrot pieces.

The man had indeed been bustin' his carrots.

I go upstairs and knock on the door. The upset tenant looks sheepish and apologizes for his outburst. He explains that he'd come back from the wholesale store to find a rejection letter in the mail from a local college where he'd applied for a program. In frustration, he opened the large bag of carrots he'd just bought and began breaking them into pieces. He admits there might have been some yelling of obscenities at this point. The scene had seemed bizarre enough to his neighbour to warrant a call to the police.

I tell him I think that's an interesting way of dealing with stress, but suggest next time he might want to bust his carrots in the privacy of his own home.

By the time I slip the car into gear, another call has come in—another neighbourly complaint. This time, one person is disturbed by a neighbour who's been watching her out the window. I can't believe, sometimes, the things people call the police about, but I have to attend. As I drive over, I realize I'm trembling a little, and I wonder if I'm still shaken from witnessing that family's grief or if I'm just starving.

The woman who called is upset because she keeps catching the lady next door staring at her as she comes and goes. I walk over to have a talk with the gawking neighbour. I'm hoping for a simple explanation; I'm hoping she will just agree to avert her eyes and stop freaking out her neighbour.

But it's not that simple. The woman next door says she has been staring—and for good reason. Over the past couple of weeks, she's heard her neighbour screaming at her kid. One day she looked out and saw our caller grab her two-year-old son by his arm, shriek "fucking little bastard," throw him into the car, and drive off without securing him in his car seat. The neighbour notified Children and Families, but since she has an ongoing file with them herself, they dismissed her. Yesterday she watched as her neighbour brought home groceries and went into the house. The two-year-old wasn't with her, so the woman thinks he was probably at home alone, napping while his mom went out to the store. Now the woman plans to keep watch, trying to gather more information or, at the very least, hoping that her vigilant observation will make her neighbour think twice about throwing her little boy into the car or leaving him home alone.

You never can tell. What starts out sounding like a completely ridiculous call can turn into a very valid reason for police intervention.

I have to contact Children and Families and ask them to launch an investigation. It's up to a social worker to determine if there is need to protect the child, to remove him from the home until it's safe for him to return.

I take a statement from this neighbour, and then I go looking for anyone else nearby who might have seen any similar incidents.

Eight hours into my shift, and I still haven't completed the interviews or processed the information from the owners of all those burglarized cars. I also haven't connected with my zone mate, who's been off tackling calls of his own.

Out here, we do keep tabs on each other. We're constantly monitoring other members as best we can, offering help if someone needs it and we're available. We especially keep our ears open for a 10-33, the call that means officer in distress.

I get in touch with my zone partner, and he agrees to meet me for a quick bite. Sometimes we go all day without stopping to eat, grateful for that crumbling granola bar at the bottom of a kit bag. When we do get a chance to stop, we aim for a place with counter service, a place where we can get our food fast in case we get called away again. We all know how it feels to sit down in a restaurant, order, and have to leave before the food makes it to the table.

At 4 p.m., my partner and I meet at a Tim Horton's and take a seat by the window with our orders. Before we even dig in, we hear "cops in the donut shop." It's two grown men speaking just loud enough for us to hear. Two men who have all the time in the world to sit in a coffee shop and call us lazy, who assume we have nothing else to do. We have a hundred other things to do, but we do need to eat.

While we finish our coffee, we tell each other the stories of our day. We skim over the hardest parts, and I save bustin' carrots for the last. I know it's good for a laugh.

In the remaining few hours of my shift, I plan to stop by the hospital to check on the accident victims, get back to the paperwork from the car thefts, and leave one last message for the social worker dealing with the nosy neighbour and the possible abuse or neglect she's witnessed. But as we're about to leave the coffee shop parking lot, we get a call about a domestic dispute, so we head over in tandem. An officer doesn't enter a domestic dispute situation alone. It's a safety issue. Domestic disputes tend to be emotionally fiery, and that makes them particularly dangerous.

Again, the call came in from a neighbour, a nearby woman who heard the screaming. When we arrive, it's quiet, but we find both the husband and wife there. I go inside to speak with her while my partner has a chat with the man outside. We keep each other in the line of sight, though.

Inside, the woman says there was no assault and no physical violence, just a lot of noise. She had opened the credit-card bill and lost her temper when she saw the outstanding balance, the purchases her unemployed husband had made over the past month. She tells me they have the same blow up once a month, every month, when the credit-card bill arrives and that she's increasingly frustrated that he won't respect her pleas to stop spending so much. With two uniformed police officers standing at her house now, she realizes it's probably time to take action, to cancel the card and restrict his access to her funds. It's an obvious solution, though perhaps one that will come with its own level of conflict.

Meanwhile, her husband is outside chatting with my partner, giving almost the same story. He tells my partner they have this big blow up about once a month, every month. I can see my partner nodding with understanding, as if to say, "Once a month. Yeah, I get that."

We've both established that nothing criminal has occurred, and that no one fears for their safety. No threats have been made. Neither of them wants help to leave the residence, so we walk back to our cars.

My partner is convinced that PMS caused the argument. He's a funny sort of fellow who likes to blame PMS for every incident that involves women—and after all, the guy told him it happened like this every month, though he failed, it seems, to mention the monthly credit-card bill, his out-of-control spending habits, and the fact that she's the only one bringing home an income. So I fill my partner in on all of that. He's laughs good-naturedly and holds to his original diagnosis: PMS.

For as long as I've worked with him, that's been his final ruling.

Maybe I should be offended, but I'm not. Coming from him, it's just a joke. I've never heard him say anything in a derogatory manner, and he treats everyone with the same respect and care that he showed this couple. Still, I stick to my guns: it was the credit-card bill.

I'm just happy to leave a domestic dispute knowing no one is hurt, and I'm glad my last call of the day isn't a hard one or one that will involve a lot of paperwork.

It's coming up on 7 p.m., and there's just enough time to fill the car with gas, get back to the office, and turn in our files for the day. By the time I've searched the car, handed in my files, changed and locked up my uniform and gun, it's almost 7:30.

I haven't had a minute to get through any of my paperwork. I haven't thoroughly documented the calls I went on today, let alone even looked at the many SUI files I'm carrying from previous shifts. It will all have to wait, and so will the people whose cars were broken into last night, the ones I didn't get to.

There's always tomorrow, I think, though I know it will bring its own challenges. Tomorrow will have its share of calls, and everything will slip just a little further behind.

When we have enough members working, we usually get time to catch up on some paperwork, but if we don't, the days rush by like this, the frustration builds, and there's always the looming possibility that a supervisor will deliver a reprimand about overdue paperwork. I think it's because some bosses have been off the road so long they've forgotten how it can be, how bogged down you can get.

I want to give the public the service they deserve; I hate letting them down, not getting all their cases in order. I can imagine how frustrating it is for the people who are waiting for information so they can file their insurance claims. Or worse, for social workers who need some paperwork so they can intervene and protect a child from one more day of mistreatment, so they can get help for a family in distress. So many things can't wait, but they must because my shift is over, and I have to push my emotions to the back of my mind and get home to my husband and my kids.

In just eleven hours, I have to come back and do it all again.

Working Short

9

Beneath the detachment office was a block of cells where prisoners were held, usually for less than twenty-four hours. There were a lot of reasons to be a prisoner there: an outstanding warrant, an ongoing investigation in which charges hadn't been laid, a determination of drunk in public.

For forty-eight hours each week, Wayne was down there in the cellblock.

Wayne looked after the male prisoners (female prisoners were held at the far end of the block and guarded by a woman who still bore the antiquated title of *matron*). He was very good at his job. His annual assessments were positive, his bosses thought highly of him, and most importantly, many of the prisoners did, too. We'd be out walking in downtown Nanaimo and some stranger would come over to shake Wayne's hand and thank him for the compassion he'd showed during the man's detention. The man would say something like, "I was having a rough time, and you were good to me."

That kind of thing happened regularly. One former prisoner even told Wayne he'd been suicidal the night he was arrested, but Wayne had stood outside his cell, talking with him, and it had saved his life. That cellblock conversation encouraged the man to make changes, to get the help he needed. To see that man alive and well, thanking Wayne for being so instrumental in turning his life around, brought tears to my eyes.

Still, it was a tough environment to work in. Wayne might call home to ask something late in the evening and in the background, I would hear a prisoner bellowing. Hours later, Wayne would call back to say goodnight, and the screaming would still be going on. And Wayne would come home and tell me that racket had carried on for much of the night, but that in the morning, sober, the prisoner had wanted to shake Wayne's hand and thank him for being so kind.

While Wayne's relationship with most of the men in his charge was one of mutual respect, he didn't always get the respect I felt he deserved from the RCMP. He was, after all, an outsider, just a municipal employee in the police station. Most of the members were friendly, but some of the guys taunted him about being a lowly guard, and Wayne took it hard. He said it made him feel like a second-class citizen at work.

A MALE OFFICER CALLED DURING one morning briefing to say he'd be late—his wife was also working, and he had to wait for a babysitter to come take charge of his young son. The watch commander hung up the phone, wriggled his pencil-thin mustache like he was thinking hard, and relayed the message to those of us assembled around the briefing table. Then he focused his attention on me, the only female at the table. "I know, Janet. You go over to his house and look after his kid so he can come to work. Go do what you women do best, and let the men come in and do the real work."

I pressed my lips together and forced them into a smile. Say nothing, I reminded myself, just get on with the day.

A few of the other members laughed. I worried that this watch commander, who was clearly no fan of having women work in the RCMP, used his position to sway junior members to his way of thinking. There was always some new guy giving him a ride to work and laughing hard at his jokes.

But being down one more man was no laughing matter. At briefing, we often discovered we had fewer than the minimum number of members allowed for a shift. The minimums are set according to meaningful factors like population and local crime statistics, but that didn't impress this particular watch commander. He'd been so long off the streets, so long sitting and sagging at his desk, that he'd forgotten what it was like to be out there, so he usually refused to call in additional manpower on overtime. It was a money-saving issue for management—the watch commander was struggling for a promotion, and keeping the budget on track is a crucial performance indicator. So is protecting the members working under your watch, of course, but this particular boss favoured a wait-and-see approach. He held off calling someone in until things really got hectic.

I got in the habit of recording the manpower shortages in my notebooks. Over and over for a period of years, there are notations like "below minimum staffing," and "7 members, min number 10. Requested watch commander call people in. Request refused." In one instance, we had three members working across two zones—that's three police officers responsible for the public safety of at least 50,000 people in each zone—and the safety of each other, too. We requested extra bodies that time, but our plea was ignored. Budgetary restraint was the priority.

During this period, I kept telling Wayne that if anything happened to me at work, if I was injured or killed, he had to grab my notebooks fast and keep them for the coroner's inquest. I wanted management to have to answer for risking our lives.

THE WATCH COMMANDER AND THE sergeant were a destructive duo, and the climate in our detachment had taken a turn for the worse under their leadership. The sergeant was relentless. In addition to overt advances like offering to slide his hands into my pockets to look for change, he delivered a steady stream of sexual suggestion. When he heard me mention an attractive black man to the switchboard operator in casual conversation, he left a piece of a vacuum hose in my file cubby. Then he cocked his shiny head and asked if I'd found his present: "It's long, black, and thick, and you can take it home and have a little fun with it," he sneered.

Another time, I found a rubber dildo with my files.

I took pictures of the vacuum hose and the dildo—at least they were something tangible and recordable—but I didn't feel I had any other recourse. I worked under the sergeant, and he answered to the watch commander who was no fan of mine and not interested in cracking down on sexual harassment. I knew that because once the sergeant and I were standing in the watch commander's office when the sergeant sidled right up beside me and asked if I liked it on top. His boss, the watch commander, glanced up from this paperwork, puckered his mouth into a disapproving pile under that little mustache, and ordered us both out of his office.

"If you're going to talk to her like that, I don't want to be a witness to anything," he simply stated. "Go do it somewhere else."

By then, I was so discouraged and so inured that I couldn't even register any surprise.

Wayne knew about all of this, and it bothered him, but there was nothing he could say or do about it. He was an outsider at the detachment—necessary, but not necessarily one of the crowd. He just had to put up with having his wife demeaned.

I know it bothered some of the male officers, too. Leaving the shift at night, one of them said to me, "It may be none of my business, but you don't have to put up with that bullshit." It was an unusual thing to say—"Just walk away" or "Let it go, forget about it" were far more typical comments—and it was naive. I did have to put up with it.

My bad attitude about the sergeant's sexual advances wasn't helping my career. While other officers were encouraged to upgrade their skills through training, and sent on interesting and useful courses, my boss said I hadn't "earned" that opportunity. He denied my request for training.

Wayne called me at work, frantic. He'd been dusting and had left the room for just a minute, leaving Erin, by then mobile, alone. When he came back, she had the nozzle end of the Pledge spray can in her mouth. He couldn't tell if she'd ingested any of the chemical, and he didn't know what to do. I told him to get off the phone with me and call Poison Control. But the woman who answered was too stunned by the scenario he'd described to offer immediate assistance. She actually interrupted him to say, "Let me get this straight—you're at home looking after your eight-month-old daughter, your wife is at work, and you're dusting?" Wayne said yes, and before he could continue, she broke in again, "Please hold. I've got to tell the girls this one!"

Soon she came back on the line and told him Erin would likely be fine, that there was little chance she'd engaged the spray and actually ingested any of the furniture polish. But she said if he had any doubts, he really should take her to the hospital and have her checked out. Erin did seem fine, but he took her in anyway and called to let me know.

I knew he was in for a wait at the hospital. I offered to pick up coffee and meet him at emergency on my break, but Wayne would have none of it. I couldn't figure out why not—why he wouldn't want my company—until he said, "Janet, think about it. I'm sitting in the waiting room at the emergency ward with a baby and a cop sitting next to me. Don't you dare show up here."

So I stayed away. Erin was absolutely fine, and our furniture looked great.

THE STOMACH FLU WAS GOING around, the way it does, and it hit Wayne hard. I had to leave him at home with two little kids and a bucket beside the bed to get to my shift. Once our briefing began and it was clear there were more than enough members to cover, I told the watch commander the situation I'd left at home and asked if I could take the night off. He let me go.

The following week, a junior member's wife came down with the same flu, and he also took time off. This member happened to be the latest ride to work for the watch commander, who always had one of the junior members pick him up. They were either intimidated by him or trying to impress him, and he was either testing their loyalty or just very reluctant to buy a second vehicle.

Shortly after the stomach flu relented, I checked the book where we logged our leave and something struck me as strange. I'd been docked twelve hours of annual leave for the one shift I'd missed, which I'd expected. The man with the sick wife had taken off two shifts, but he hadn't been docked at all. When I asked the watch commander about it, he said the member had applied for and received compassionate leave because his wife was ill. I consulted the policy and realized I qualified for compassionate leave, too—but only the officer in charge of the detachment could approve it. I went to the junior member and asked, innocently enough, how he'd gone about getting the time approved, just who he had submitted his memo to. He looked at me strangely, shrugged, and said he hadn't filed any memo—

the watch commander had just given him the time.

In accordance with policy, I prepared a memo to the officer in charge—the watch commander's boss. In it, I didn't just ask for compassionate leave, I also asked why another member who'd missed work for the exact same reason was given leave by the watch commander. I wondered if there were different rules for different people, and if that difference might have something to do with gender.

My compassionate leave was approved and the time returned to my leave bank, but my insolence won me another closed-door session and an angry warning from the watch commander never to go over his head again. By then I'd had enough of keeping quiet, and I thought I'd found a fissure in the system, some small opening I could use to expose the fundamental unfairness of the system. I pointed out that I'd followed the procedure he'd outlined for me—if he got in trouble for giving hours away to his favourites, well that wasn't my fault.

My tactics and my refusal to back down didn't do much to boost my popularity with him, and now I'd put myself on the radar of the officer in charge, a man I sensed also didn't have any great fondness for a loud-mouthed woman. Instead of opening a space in the system to address unfairness, I had just found another unpleasant, hard spot to wedge myself into, and another way to mark myself as unwanted in the detachment.

Once a week, on Wednesday nights, some of the moms from the school met in a portable classroom for a group they called "Stitch." They worked on whatever crafting project they had going: knitting or cross stitch, rug hooking or scrap booking. When I found out, I wanted to go, but I was hesitant. People sometimes don't like female cops or they have strange reactions to police officers in general and hold them apart, as if getting to know someone whose job is law enforcement is the same as getting tangled up with the law.

Still, I loved to knit and had tried my hand at cross stitch and sewing, and I was hungry for some crafty distraction. I took a deep breath and showed up one Wednesday night. To my surprise and relief, the group welcomed me with open arms.

Since everybody was working on something different, something all their own, it wasn't a how-to. There was no competition. There were just pots of tea and coffee and lots of conversation about life—about spouses and kids, parents and work, and whatever else someone felt the need to discuss. The women were always pleasant, always willing to listen and offer advice or just support. Some nights they would put aside their problems to listen to somebody else who needed to vent. No matter what the drama, we always had a good time, and we always ended with, "See you next week!"

One Wednesday night turned into fifteen years of Wednesday nights. I couldn't always make it because of my work schedule, but I endeavoured to go as often as I could.

It was a fluid group with a core of about seven women, while others came and went. We celebrated each other. For birthdays, someone brought a cake, and our crafting guru, Tania, made a card we all could sign. As our children grew, there were more and more milestones to mark: graduations, grandchildren, first jobs, first dates, broken hearts. Over the years, each woman in that group had their share of joy and of calamity. Every Wednesday night the conversation took an interesting turn as someone sought parenting advice or marital advice or vented about some new illustration of life's fundamental unfairness. Eventually, of course, we came to laughingly call the group "Stitch & Bitch."

When things got bad in the RCMP and worse at home, the group was my salvation. They listened to my stories, heard me complain, and watched me cry. They offered comfort, and they worried about me when I didn't show up.

IT WAS EARLY EVENING, VERY near the end of shift and getting dark, and we were working below the minimum number. I was alone in North Zone when the calls started coming in from an apartment building where a young woman was taking a pounding. She was running through the halls, trying to escape her assailant. The callers reported that the man was out of control, that when he caught her, he'd smash her head against the concrete walls. I sat outside the building in my car, listening to the updates with my teeth clenched. I couldn't go in alone. I had to wait for backup to come from across the city.

When that backup finally arrived—and I know he came as fast as he could—we rushed in and cornered the suspect in a narrow hallway. He was crazed, high on something besides just the adrenaline, and both the other officer and I pulled out our pepper spray to subdue him. In that confined space I think we took as much of the spray in the blowback as the suspect did, but we were able to get him under control and find the victim, who was badly injured. Two ambulances showed up, thank God. One rushed the young woman to the hospital, and the paramedics in the other washed out our eyes and gave us some relief from the burning after-effects of pepper spray.

Leaving that scene, I was keenly aware that if there'd been more officers on the job, we could have saved that girl some severe head trauma. I was mad as hell about it and no way was I keeping it to myself. Back at the office, I marched straight to the watch commander's office, and I told him he was going to get someone killed running the watch so short. It's possible, with all the adrenaline in my system, that I was yelling. But why wouldn't I? I'd just come from a call where a woman had her head bashed in while I sat outside, powerless to intervene. I'd just been pepper sprayed, and my eyes and lungs were still on fire.

I didn't care how unimpressed the watch commander was with my tone, and I didn't anticipate what would happen next. Within days, I was hauled into a staffing interview—at least that's what I was told it was. They'd brought a staffing officer over to Nanaimo for it. Staffing interviews occur when an officer is in shit or is performing below standards. I'd never had any memos or notices about problems with my performance, so I figured this must be retaliation. And it was savage. The "interviewer," a man I'd never seen before, didn't ask many questions. Instead, he spent about an hour telling me that I wasn't welcome in the detachment anymore, that I was despised in Nanaimo, and that I didn't pull my weight. I was reeling, and I remember asking him who he'd spoken to about me. Other officers? Staff in the radio room? He wouldn't tell me.

It was awful, being berated and bullied like that, having to wonder who hated me, who I had let down, who among my co-workers thought I was a doing a bad job. Did everyone in the detachment really have such a low opinion of me? Did everyone want me gone?

That day, I went home in tears, and I tried to explain through my sobs what had happened, how over and over again I'd been told I was a lousy cop. Wayne did his best to reassure me, and then he got mad. He was livid about how I was being treated, but of course he was as powerless as I was. He couldn't do anything to defend me that wouldn't compromise his ability to do his own job. He just had to go into work and get along with the bullies who had turned his wife into a sobbing mess.

I hoped the report of my staffing interview—there's a form that has to be completed and placed in the member's file—would shed some light on things, give me a clue about who had said what, who hated me and why. I waited nervously for the report, but no report was filed. Ever. There's no record that a staffing interview with me was ever conducted. After a while, I asked the sergeant why I'd received no written record. He leaned over and whispered, "Because that was an attempt to get you to quit."

I WANTED MY DAUGHTERS TO share my love of the outdoors. I would beg Wayne to come camping with us, but he always chose to stay home. He said there was nothing for him to do on a camping trip. I'd run through the list—hiking the trails, playing Frisbee on the beach, or building a sandcastle with your kids. What about enjoying a campfire at night with your wife? He just wasn't interested in making those kinds of memories. Once, I successfully cajoled him into coming along, but he only made it one night. On the morning of the second day, I drove him to catch a bus home. He claimed he didn't work all year to go out for a week and pretend he was homeless. After that, the girls and I planned an annual camping trip without him.

We always went to the staggeringly beautiful west coast of Vancouver Island where, just outside Tofino, the sand stretches for miles. We'd get a campsite right on the bluff above the waves at Mackenzie Beach and spend our days swimming, gathering driftwood, examining the tide pools, and embracing whatever nature had to offer. At night, we'd build a campfire and eat s'mores. Torrential rains would douse us, but we loved lying in a tent and listening to the waves crash and the rain pound down on the tarp above our heads.

So much detritus piled up inside me over the year, but Tofino's thundering waves never failed to wash away some of the clutter in my head.

AT WORK, I HAD NOTHING left to lose. I was already despised as "a fucking woman with a big mouth" by my superiors, so I opened it again. I told the watch commander that I jotted in my notebooks how many officers were on shift and kept track of his refusals to call in overtime officers when requested. He was furious that I was trying to compel him to comply with regulations, but it made a difference. Suddenly, he was willing to staff up.

For me, though, the battle at work had become so exhausting, so stressful, that the anticipation of going in made me physically ill. There were days when I was puking at home before my shift. Wayne would often call in on my behalf because I just couldn't bring myself to do it. It wasn't the policing that had me unnerved—I never lost my nerve for going out on the road. It was walking through the doors and into that police station I couldn't face.

Years later, looking back through my notebooks from this period, I noticed a disturbing pattern. During the time both the sexual harassment and the overarching sense of hostility were at their worst, the number of sick days I took went through the roof. My notebook is littered with ODS—Off Duty Sick. Usually it was the first day shift of the four-shift block that I missed. No matter how bad I felt, I tried never to miss two shifts in a row since that would leave my watch mates tired and scrambling while my files fell further behind. The guilt over letting my colleagues down only compounded how terrible I felt.

But there was something else about those notations, something I hadn't been aware of at the time. Usually, when I had occasion to call in sick, I entered a reason in my notebook in case I needed to remember it later. Those entries read, "ODS: ear infection," or "ODS: stomach flu." Specifics like that occur in my earlier notebooks and return in notebooks after we had a change of management in Nanaimo. But during the time I had so many first day-shift absences, when I was sick with anxiety, I would simply enter "ODS." I suppose I felt I couldn't enter an explanation, that if my notebook were needed as an official document in court, it shouldn't contain lines like "ODS: puking because I dread work," or "ODS: too anxious to sleep because watch commander due back from holidays."

I was worried about my credibility in court. But in hindsight, I should have entered the reasons I was too sick to work. It would have served me well later—served as some small proof that this all happened.

We didn't talk to Ashley and Erin about the things we saw at our jobs. They were far too young to hear the ugly and sad details. If they asked me, "What did you do today, Mommy?" I just said, "Not much. Tell me all about your day." We talked about school and what we should have for dinner, and sometimes we all took the dog for a walk together in the evening.

But as things got thornier at work, Wayne and I did air our frustrations at home. What started as the occasional gripe session about office politics escalated into a daily dissection of the gossip, the back stabbing, and the wrongs we'd witnessed. It became the biggest part of our communication, and it was telling, how the dynamics with and between our co-workers affected us more than any of the tragedies we dealt with in our jobs. We sought understanding, validation from each other that what we were experiencing was not right. I think we were looking for affirmation that, despite the craziness, we were both okay.

But after a while, I began to worry our conversations would impact the girls' outlook toward their own careers. I didn't want them to grow up hating the idea of going to work because of what they'd overheard at home. I wanted them to have a strong work ethic; I wanted them to know that jobs could be wonderful and challenging. So I put a stop to those conversations. I decided we shouldn't spend our time together discussing the evils at work.

Unfortunately, Wayne misunderstood my motivation. He saw my refusal to engage as a sign I didn't care about his issues and his frustrations, which began to build. What had been common ground soon became a point of contention. I told him he couldn't come home every day and just unload his frustrations on me—I didn't have the power to make anything better. I said he needed to take a stand with those who upset him the most. He argued that he couldn't because he was afraid of the repercussions. Of course I understood that all too well, but I'd drawn a line I felt strongly about, and besides, complaining to each other wouldn't change a thing.

FOR A WHILE, THE RCMP became heavily involved in Community Policing. It was an attempt to prevent crime through proactive work. A subset, "Problem Oriented Policing" projects—POP projects—arose out of the notion that police officers could identify specific problems in the community and develop solutions based on their first-hand experience.

One officer came up with an awareness project to make shoppers at local malls more vigilant about concealing valuables and locking their cars. Under his plan, police would check cars in the lot, lock doors that were left unlocked, and even put pre-printed notices on windshields reminding the owners to conceal new merchandise in their trunks. Another officer devised a project to encourage residents to put up more prominent house numbers and illuminate them, ensure they were highly visible. That way, emergency services could find the house faster if someone was forcing their way in or if there was a fire or a heart attack happening.

Designing and implementing these projects—or supervising the officers who did—showcased creativity and initiative in solving everyday problems, so they looked great on applications for promotion. The watch commander just happened to be seeking a promotion when he announced that everybody on our watch had to come up with a POP project, implement it, and complete a file on it.

We were already overwhelmed, overworked, and understaffed. Asking us to take on another big responsibility seemed absurd. I checked around the detachment and discovered members on the other three watches had not been told to do POP projects, so I assumed the directive had more to do with the watch commander's bid for promotion to inspector than it did with effectively policing our community.

If every member of every watch had been asked to participate, if it were a detachment-wide initiative, I would have embraced it in a heartbeat. I was a huge fan of community policing—just not on these terms. I refused. Maybe that sounds spiteful, and maybe it was, but I just wasn't about to use my valuable time to promote a man I thought was a terrible leader.

Months passed, and as the promotional process progressed, those of us working under him all received a package with a questionnaire about his leadership skills and supervisory style. The questionnaire was anonymous. At a local community station, I sat down with those papers, and I wrote out all my answers honestly. I detailed my understanding of his attitude toward women on the force, and his blatant refusal to stop a subordinate from making crude sexual comments to the officers under him. I wrote, emphatically, that I didn't think this man should have achieved his current rank, let alone be promoted to the next.

Once I was done, I sat back and thought about the consequences. If the watch commander failed in his bid to get a promotion, we were stuck with him. If I sent this in, I'd be punishing my own watch. And somehow, too, it seemed so low, so underhanded, to send in an anonymous diatribe that could kill someone else's career. I put the whole questionnaire through the shredder right then and there, before anyone else ever read it.

Some weeks later, the watch commander called me to his office. I had no idea what I'd done, but I was upset enough to stop at the washroom and vomit. Then I pulled myself together; I fixed my shirt, brushed my teeth, and headed upstairs.

He told me to close the door. When I did, he said, "Congratulations, you fucked me out of a promotion." I just looked at him, puzzled. I wasn't sure what I'd done. He went on to tell me that my assessment of him had ruined his chances for a promotion.

It was the first time I'd thought about that questionnaire since I'd shredded it.

Suddenly, I had the upper hand. I knew something he didn't. I calmly admitted that I had, in fact, criticized his leadership skills when I'd written out my answers and that nothing I'd said was favourable. And I told him that if I'd sent that questionnaire in—if I hadn't shredded the whole thing—then maybe, probably, it would have fucked him over. But I had shredded it, and so I pointed out the obvious.

"I guess I'm not the only one who feels this way about you."

I got up, and I opened the door.

Shooting Stars

10

I wasn't ambitious enough. That was the criticism in my annual assessment—the only negative assessment I'd ever had. Proof of my wanton lack of ambition was that I had not written the JSE (Job Simulation Exercise) test. The test was voluntary, open to all members who had enough years under their gun belts, and the test score played a pivotal part in whether one got promoted.

There was a push on to get more women to write the test. That's what the sergeant told me: pressure was being felt from outside forces. The RCMP was being scrutinized by other police organizations, policing experts, and criminology researchers, and it was falling short on moving women up through the ranks. To me, it seemed obvious that women within the RCMP lived with the chill of harassment and bullying and the fear of speaking out against it. I assumed many believed, as I did, that there was an old boys' club operating that did not welcome women into their fraternity. The easy solution? Blame the women for not writing a test and pursuing a more ambitious path.

But the truth is, I didn't want to get promoted. I had little faith in the management of the RCMP. Why would I want to walk among the men who had labelled me a "fucking woman with a big mouth"? I had watched as vulgar, harassing comments were brushed aside; I'd seen too many decisions made for reasons that had nothing to do with safety or effective policing. I wanted no part in that higher echelon.

Of course, I had other reasons for not wanting to rise through the ranks at that stage of my life. I wrote a rebuttal to the comments in my assessment, explaining that with two young children at home, elderly in-laws who needed support, and a spouse who also worked shift work, my time and energy were spread thinly enough. I suggested my supervisor spend a month in my shoes before criticizing my lack of ambition. Besides, I said, I enjoyed working with the public as a constable. I pointed out that not every nurse at the hospital aspires to head nurse, and not every electrician at the mill wants to be the boss. I thought they should respect the fact that I knew my current limitations and knew I couldn't give a management position the dedication it deserved at this time.

Instead, I was reprimanded for my rebuttal and told never to negatively comment on something a superior wrote in an assessment. I was warned about being flagged as a troublemaker, warned that my career was essentially over. By then, I didn't care.

The performance assessments that mattered most to me came from outside the force anyway, from women like Mary.

At Pipers Lagoon, the water comes and goes with the tides, and children love to explore the beaches and bluffs. It's one of Nanaimo's most beautiful parks, and maybe that's why it's the place Mary chose to end her life in 2000. She was found unconscious and nearly frozen to death in the early hours of the morning, her pants around her ankles. No identification. We had no idea what had happened to this mystery woman in her fifties.

At the hospital, they gradually raised her core body temperature and determined she had taken an overdose of a prescription medication, but she was still unconscious. There was an unclaimed car in the parking lot at Pipers Lagoon, registered to a man. I'd gone by the address on the registration, but as no one was home, I went to the hospital and waited for her to wake up. I stayed at her bedside. This woman had felt lonely and desperate enough to want to die. I didn't want her to wake up alone in a hospital.

When she came to, we talked. She told me she hadn't wanted to die, not really, but she'd felt powerless to change her life and saw no other way to go. Her husband later came to the hospital. He acknowledged some marital discord and told me he'd understood that she was depressed, but he hadn't realized just how bad it was.

For years after that, every once in a while, Mary sent a card to me at the police station expressing her gratitude toward all the emergency workers who'd saved her life. She and her husband had worked on things together, had found a happier place, and now there were grandchildren and all kinds of reasons to live.

Ashley and Erin were close to their Nana and Papa Merlo, and they were very accustomed to hospital visits. We kept a backpack ready, full of things to occupy the kids, while we visited one or the other of their grandparents. Broken bones, heart bypasses, aneurysms, congestive heart failure—Wayne, Jeannie, and I did what we could to look after Jack and Kay through all the complications of their physical decline. And the girls tuned in from a young age; they grew up acutely aware of the frailty of other people and the need to hold a door or notice someone who was struggling and help them out.

Fortunately, while Jack and Kay suffered physically, their

spirits stayed strong. Our girls were always guaranteed a good time at their grandparents, and the bond between them was solid. Kay bought hilarious toys. I remember a battery-operated flower that danced when you sang to it. The kids loved it, and Kay loved watching them carry on (though of course there were days, in the middle of all that carrying on, when Wayne and I would hit our load limit). I'm convinced that having her exuberant granddaughters in her life kept Kay alive long after the doctors thought she'd be gone.

I took a turn at convalescing when the girls were young, too. After years of suffering with endometriosis, I had a routine hysterectomy. Everything seemed fine until a week after my surgery, when Wayne came home to find me curled on the couch. It was the height of summer, stifling outside, and I was in flannel pajamas, freezing, my temperature sky high, and a searing pain cutting across my middle. I'd developed a post-op wound infection. At the hospital, they reopened the incision to clean it out and dosed me with intravenous antibiotics. For months afterward, a nurse would have to come to our house and pack, cauterize, and re-bandage my wound. It was a mess, and it had to heal from the inside out—a long process. I was off work for six months, and then had to do a gradual return to full service. Because I'd lost so much core muscle strength, I had trouble sitting for any length of time, and I could only bear my heavy gun belt for short intervals.

When I got back to work, I found a copy of an email with my files. The staff sergeant had submitted my name to write the JSE exam, the voluntary test I'd been adamant about not taking. He'd signed me up in my absence, never even consulted me. The exam date was just days away. I came across a confirmation email and a map of the university campus with directions for where to go to write the test I didn't want to take and was utterly unprepared to pass. According to the instructions, it could take up to four hours to complete—far longer than I could sit at a desk without pain.

I was trapped. I knew I wouldn't succeed if I tried to take the test, and I knew if I failed to write it, I'd be criticized again in my annual assessment. There was no way to do anything right.

So on test day, I didn't bother to show up.

ERIN AND ASHLEY WERE EASY kids. Their teachers always commented on how good they were, and even strangers complimented their manners. But while they were learning to be polite, I wanted them to learn to respect themselves, too, so from a very young age I treated them with respect. I talked to them, and if they misbehaved, I made sure to explain what they'd done wrong.

In the time I had available, I tried to give them a broad appreciation of the world. I read to them a lot, and because they were as interested in doing crafts as I was, we spent hours colouring, creating beautiful things, casting moulds, and painting figurines. I wanted to engage their creative sides, to let them think freely and dream big. I wanted to give myself some time to experience joy.

For Wayne, joy meant trains. He knew intricate details of every type of locomotive. For years he had collected train books, magazines, and memorabilia, and eventually, he began to collect brass replica locomotives built to one-sixteenth scale. With that collection, his fondness for trains turned to more of an obsession. Our day trips started to involve trains—if there was a train museum, a train ride, or a train worth seeing, we were going there. And before long, every family outing had a train theme.

I should have been sympathetic to how much stress he was under, realized that his hobby was therapeutic. Instead, I began to resent it. When the train show was on at the local community center, it was an annual must-attend event for all of us. But when there was a craft fair at the same facility, not only did Wayne not wish to go, but he didn't want me to attend either. He didn't want to drive me there and he didn't want me parking the car there because someone might open a door into it and leave a dent. Sometimes I tried to insist, but more often I acquiesced.

Maybe I should have tried harder, but I was so disheartened from trying to do my job well while being constantly harassed or disrespected at work, so exhausted by busy kids and family turmoil, that I could only fight battles on so many fronts.

A HANDFUL OF THE GUYS at work were going fishing out in the middle of nowhere in early March. To me, it sounded like a great way to spend a few days off, to reacquaint myself with my colleagues after such a long absence. The place we went was isolated and serene. No bosses, no public, no computer or television, and no phone. There was barely even a cellphone signal, but that's how a friend finally got through to me, on my cell.

We were out in the boat—out on the ocean, fishing—and she was calling to see if I was okay. Four RCMP officers, she told me, had been gunned down. All of them were dead. That's all she knew; she didn't know where they were from.

We raced back to shore and everybody was trying to get calls through, to find out some more information. All of us frantic. Even after we learned they were in Alberta and we learned their names and we didn't know them, we were still gutted.

I had such a profound sense of loss about the tragedy at Mayerthorpe. Despite the issues I had with some officers and especially with my immediate superiors, the RCMP was like an extended family. We were all in it together, and when those members were gunned down, it felt like members of my own family had been murdered.

THERE WAS TALK AROUND THE office about transfers coming for those who'd been in town more than ten years. Word was the moves were necessary to accommodate members who'd been posted in Canada's north and now were asking to come back to a larger center. Nanaimo had been requested, and I wholeheartedly agreed that someone who'd made the sacrifice to go to an isolated location should get the posting they wanted next.

If I had to leave Nanaimo and commute to some other detachment, we could make it work. Wayne, of course, was a municipal employee and didn't have the flexibility to go; his career and his pension were tied up in Nanaimo, and his parents needed him nearby. But there were plenty of detachments within easy commuting distance. It would be good for me—and good for my career—to get out of Nanaimo. I'd had enough of the harassment, the favouritism, and the games. I couldn't keep my mouth shut anymore, and I'd learned that speaking out, or trying to shine a light into a dark secret, just led to nasty outcomes.

Once, at a difficult time, all that was sustaining me was the planning and preparation for my annual camping trip with the girls. I knew the roar of the waves would wash away some of my constant worry, and the salt air would bring me back to myself. I'd recently taken a stand and been particularly vocal about wrongdoing. Then just days before we were supposed to leave for Tofino, my long-scheduled vacation was suddenly cancelled by my boss at the RCMP. He expressed a newfound interest in not having the detachment work short of officers, though I suspected his decision had more to do with how recently I'd stood up to him. The words felt good coming out my mouth, but a week on the beach with my girls would have been much more fulfilling. I was alternately furious—with him and with myself—and devastated, but I had no proof of his motives and no recourse, so I clamped my lips together at work. And at home, I apologized profusely to Ashley and Erin.

I HAD A KNACK FOR meeting people in weird ways and turning chance encounters into close friendships. Among my confidantes was a man named David, a Wisconsin farmer I'd met, ironically, online in the early days of the Internet when I'd visited chat rooms to assess the dangers of cyber-predators. David became a close friend and part of the elaborate support system that kept me afloat.

I met another friend at a local tire shop. I was waiting while they put the snow tires on my police car when a big, burly man approached me. He didn't look hostile, but I was on my guard, expecting him to make some comment about the size of me, standing there in my uniform. Instead, he asked, "What kind of engine do you have in that police car?" I guess he expected me to know a thing like that, but I had no clue.

He laughed. He had a thick thatch of beard and piercing blue eyes, and his expression said he thought I might be a complete idiot, but he didn't walk away. He just changed the subject, and we had a nice chat while we waited for our vehicles. A few weeks later, the first snowfall put those tires to work. There was a lull in the action at about four in the morning. I was sitting in my police car, watching the snow fall, and catching up on some paperwork when a 4x4 pulled up next to me. It was the same burly guy.

He called out, "Are you stuck?" I assured him I was fine, but he didn't drive away. Instead, he introduced himself—Mike O'Hanley—and explained that his dog always got him up early. The dog, Attu, was also enormous. It was a long-haired wolf and German shepherd mix, and on its hind legs, the thing would have stood taller than me. No doubt it outweighed me, too.

Every early morning, Mike took Attu for a walk around the park, and when I was working nights and had time, I'd bring coffee, and we'd stand and talk while Attu ran around. You meet all kinds in the wee hours of the morning, but few of them are as smart, funny, and wise as Mike. In this huge man, always dressed in a plaid jacket and sweatpants, I found a surrogate big brother. Standing in that park at sunrise, I discovered I could confide in him all the things I'd been trying to keep inside—the struggles I was having at home and the ongoing battles at work. Mike just listened and never passed judgment, and if it got too heavy, he threw in a corny joke to lighten the mood.

One night, Mike called and told me to pick up some coffee and meet him when I could in a very remote, wooded area. It was a place I often patrolled looking for stolen cars and drinking teenagers. He didn't tell me what was going on, and when I arrived, it was quiet and dark. No teenagers, no sign of any trouble. I used my flashlight to locate Mike, standing in that utter darkness, handed him his coffee, and asked what the hell he was doing out in the middle of nowhere.

He said, "Be quiet and look up," and he pointed to the sky.

It was a meteor shower. Shooting stars soared across the sky. We stood in awestruck silence, and then Mike asked some simple question. When I looked over to answer him, he said, "Dammit, you missed one. Pay attention." He pointed me back to the sky. Before long, I turned to say something else, and he told me I'd missed another shooting star. For a long time after that night, he joked that I was always so busy talking I was destined to miss the biggest and the best shooting stars of my life.

Coming Apart

11

The driver lost control of the car near an intersection on the new Nanaimo Parkway. When the car rammed the guardrail separating the lanes of traffic, it was still travelling at top highway speeds. The passenger side took the full brunt of metal and concrete before the car went airborne, flipped, and landed on its roof.

When I arrived, it was resting in the southbound lane well beyond the reach of the streetlights at the nearby intersection, shrouded in darkness. Rain was coming down in sheets. We were working short that night, and I was the only one out in my zone, so I was alone on the scene, hoping the ambulance and the fire department would arrive quickly. I was afraid an oncoming car would crash into the wreckage, but all I could do, out there by myself, was park my car across the road like a buffer, the lights strobing, and hope for the best.

I was soaked to the skin before I even got to the wreck, but I wasn't thinking about that. I was checking for signs of a gasoline leak or the risk of fire. It was safe, so I crouched down on the driver's side and looked in with my flashlight. The beam illuminated the driver and one passenger, a man and a woman suspended upside down by their seatbelts, crumpled metal and shattered glass everywhere. The driver was conscious, coherent, and his only concern was his passenger.

I ran around to check on her, laid flat on my belly and peered in. She was covered in blood, badly mangled, and her head was strangely twisted sideways, so I couldn't see her face, just her wavy blonde hair. The driver yelled out, asking if she was alive, if she was going to be okay. I could hear her laboured breathing as I reached in, searching for a pulse. I told him yes, she was alive. I didn't say how bad she was hurt, but he knew.

He was trapped. He couldn't move, couldn't get out, and couldn't reach out to her. He could hear her though, over the drumming downpour. Even to the uninitiated, the sound coming from her was unmistakeable. Unmistakeable and unforgettable. It was the desperate rattle of breath going in that's doing no good, and it seemed as loud as thunder in the dark.

No ambulance, no firemen, no other police yet. Just me.

The driver asked me to hold her hand. "Please don't let her die alone," he begged. I found her hand and I cradled it. I said the kinds of things you say—"It's going to be okay," and "Help is on the way." I didn't want her to be scared. We'd been told so many times that the last sense to go when a person dies is their hearing, and I wanted the last thing she heard to be a soothing voice. Rain hammered on the car and ran down my neck and back, and I kept hold of her hand, placed my other hand gently on her head and talked to her until I knew she was gone.

In the distance, I could hear sirens approaching.

I WAS TOLD TO GET going on my transfer. They wanted to move me to Surrey—over on the mainland, just outside of Vancouver. It would mean leaving home and family for nearly a week at a time and renting an apartment or some other second residence over there. It was a ridiculous request, and not one that was being made of most others. Management knew we had young children, that my husband's job was tied to Nanaimo, that his mother was chronically ill with congestive heart failure, and that his dad was terminally ill, battling kidney failure and bladder cancer. There was no way Wayne would be able to manage working his shifts at the police station and juggling care for his daughters and his elderly parents while I spent my off-hours alone in an apartment on the mainland.

Meanwhile, new recruits were showing up in Nanaimo straight out of Depot, but there was nobody coming in who'd been posted to a remote community.

I begged to move within daily commuting distance. I was told I had no choice, that, after all, I had volunteered to go. In an interview with the officer in charge of the Nanaimo detachment, I explained about the care my in-laws required. He told me, "That's what nursing homes are for."

That's when I began to write emails, to send letters to Staffing and to anybody else I thought might listen. Their responses were all the same: "You agreed to this transfer." It's true, I had. But I'd agreed under false pretenses when I believed everybody had to move out to let the people from isolated postings come in.

Wayne worked in our office, too. It was no secret we were embattled by family issues. I understood that I'd been too vocal and that they wanted to punish me, but he had never caused any trouble. He was always so respectful and compassionate towards others. Now, at this terrible time in his life, he was being denied compassion.

WHEN THE OTHER EMERGENCY SERVICES arrived at the accident on the parkway, I switched to auto pilot and did what was necessary at a fatal accident. Traffic had to be diverted, the coroner and traffic investigators called to the scene. The fire department placed wooden blocks under the car as a precaution. I didn't understand why—the car seemed stable on its roof, but that was their job, not mine. Firefighters play by a very different set of rules than police officers do.

The victims were extracted from the demolished car. The driver was taken to hospital, and once the coroner gave the go-ahead, his passenger was taken away to the morgue. A tow truck then moved in to flip the car back onto its wheels and drag it away. Rain was still slashing down. As I watched the tow truck execute its manoeuvres, one of the firemen came over and put his hand on my shoulder.

He said they were headed back to the fire hall, and he asked me to do them a favour. It was past their bedtime, he told me—firefighters have sleeping quarters in the fire hall, so they often get plenty of rest between calls—and they didn't want to have to wait the ten minutes it would take for the tow truck to get the car out of there. He wanted me to gather up the wooden blocks they'd wedged underneath and bring them over to the fire hall. Just leave them by the door, he said, so you don't wake us up. Then he laughed at how soaked I was and wished me a good night.

As soon as the car was taken from the scene, I took great pleasure in kicking those wooden supports right off the highway and down the embankment.

WAYNE FRETTED CONSTANTLY ABOUT HIS parents and drove them crazy calling to check on them several times a day. As they deteriorated and he realized he was completely powerless to change what was happening to them, Wayne began to focus his control on material things. He would run the washing machine through its full cycle, empty, after I washed clothes to ensure it was clean inside. He cleaned the dryer lint trap like it was a medical instrument. Then he used Windex on the appliances to remove fingerprints, and waxed them until they gleamed.

It only got worse from there. Eventually, he wouldn't allow me to use the washer or dryer at all for fear they would wear out. We often spent our day off at the laundromat, washing clothes. I went along because I just couldn't cope with another yelling match over the appliances. I didn't consider how shutting up was just enabling him, letting him edge into more and more outrageous behavior.

I remember someone saying one time, "You guys make good money. Why can't you afford a washer and dryer?" I was too embarrassed to admit I wasn't allowed to use the appliances at home, so I made an excuse, said it was just quicker and easier to haul it all down to the laundromat and do it at once.

Soon, Wayne's behavior extended to the refrigerator, the stove, the microwave, and our cars. Even the lawnmower and the tools were dragged into Wayne's compulsive cleaning orbit. When the postman complimented on our new Lawn Boy lawnmower, Wayne was so proud to tell him, "Nope, this is twenty years old."

As his parents got sicker and the stress at work mounted, life became like a bad dream at home. When the girls came into our room to say good morning, Wayne would reply in his deep, stern voice, "Is your room clean?" The girls would turn around and slink out. It broke my heart—repeatedly.

Before he left to walk to work, Wayne would note the kilometers on the car, and he would berate me when he got home if I'd gone out for groceries or taken the girls somewhere after school. His greeting when he walked through the door would be, "Where the fuck did you go today? You put thirty kilometers on that thing." Then I'd get a lecture on how irresponsible I was, how I was going to "run the shit out of it."

It wasn't just our car. He'd go to his parents' house and

spend an hour washing their car, then order them not to take it anywhere because it would get dirty. They caved to his demands, spending days at home to avoid the outbursts and the shouting that disagreeing with Wayne would trigger.

Once, when they'd taken the car—their own car—out, he flew into a rage, yelling until Kay was in tears. I had to wade in and make him stop, so I shouted, "That's enough."

Wayne turned on me then, his voice even louder as he called me every insulting name he could come up with. Then he stormed out and walked home.

After he was gone, Jack sunk into a chair and also began to cry. I'd never seen my father-in-law cry before. He kept apologizing for his son's treatment of me. "He has never heard me disrespect his mom like that. I want you to know he didn't learn that behaviour from me."

Jack Merlo didn't have to tell me that. I knew what kind of man he was—generous and kind, especially to his wife. I knew, too—or thought I knew—what kind of man Wayne was. But he wasn't himself. Something else, someone else, had taken him over.

THE 9-1-1 OPERATORS SAY THE worst thing about their jobs is not knowing how it all turned out. They continually deal with people in great distress, take those calls, dispatch the emergency crews, and sometimes stay on the phone for a long time with the caller. But after they hang up, the operators seldom learn the outcome of these harrowing situations. Once in awhile, when we went into the radio room at work to chat, one of the operators would ask how something had turned out. That was the extent of closure for them.

In some respects, the same holds true for a police officer. You see the collision and its immediate aftermath, but you don't always get to follow the story to a reasonable conclusion. There are just too many to follow up on.

When I left the scene of that car accident, I had the dead woman's identification, so I headed for the hospital to pass it on to the coroner. Really, I wanted to check on the status of the driver. I was so wet and so cold, I hunched over the steering wheel in my car and let my hands warm up on the air blowing from the heat vents. I didn't sit back in my seat to drive, and I didn't put on my seat belt.

In the emergency ward, the identification slipped from my hand and fell to the floor. When I bent over to pick it up, a litre of water that had been trapped in the hood of my Gore-Tex jacket spilled out and doused the back of my head and neck. It splashed all over the hospital floor and the staff laughed and asked how long I'd stood in the rain to build up such a reserve.

"A long time," I replied. A very long time.

AT THE SCENE OF A sudden death, police officers gather evidence and personal information about the victim, take pictures, and preserve the scene so an investigation can be conducted. When the death is determined to have been from natural causes, the family is notified and police involvement is over. Memories of the scene, however, aren't so easily shut down.

Before he died, the old man had been left alone for a long time. We knew as soon as we entered that he was dead—there's no mistaking the repellent smell of decay—and we knew he must have been incontinent for days before his death because the odor of decomposition was accompanied by the stench of human waste. The body was wedged between the bed and the wall as if he'd tried to get out of bed but had chosen the wrong side and fallen onto the electric baseboard with his right arm and shoulder pressed against the heater. I guess he didn't have the strength to get up, and who knows how long he was stuck there, dying.

There was no forced entry into the home. The death apparently resulted from natural causes.

We moved the body from behind the bed and laid him on the bedroom floor. As we lifted him to put him in the body bag, I grabbed his right shoulder. His whole arm came off in my hands.

When Wayne worked his graveyard shifts, the girls and I would have girls' night. We'd pop popcorn in the microwave, cuddle up on the couch, and watch a movie. If we really felt rebellious, we'd throw on a load of laundry, too. Sometimes at the last minute, Wayne would tell us he'd taken the night off, and we'd all be disappointed.

Like me, the girls longed to share a normal family evening with their dad, but it wasn't possible. Instead of watching a movie with us, he'd tell us that we were going to wear out the DVD player. We could never to go the mall, a movie, or the ski hill anymore because someone might park next to us and scratch the door on the car. Wayne's illness was strangling him, and as it did, it strangled us as well. His daughters felt displaced in his affections by his material possessions.

We all walked on eggshells. I had started sleeping with my ATM card, my credit card, and the keys to the house and car in my sock, in case Wayne freaked out in the middle of the night and I had to get out of the house. On two occasions, I'd actually taken the girls and gone to a hotel until he cooled down. I begged him to get help—his parents and Jeannie did, too—but he couldn't see that he had a problem.

Inside all that craziness, I saw a struggling lost soul. I loved him so much, and I didn't want to make things worse for any of us by fighting him on a daily basis. I still had faith that the old Wayne would come back to the wife and the daughters who missed him so desperately.

THE NIGHT I HELD THAT dying woman's hand—a night that will never leave my memory—I went back to the office and changed into dry clothes. Still chilled after that, I stopped to get some tea. As I stood at the counter waiting my turn, a table of teens close by started with the comments. They could smell bacon. There must be a pig around. I wanted to respond, but I realized nothing I could say, nothing I could tell them about my night, would make a dent in their malevolent perspectives. There was just no point.

I didn't sit down and enjoy my tea. I carried it to the car and let the dispatchers know I was ready for the next call. Please, I thought, please let the calls for the rest of the night be easy ones.

Holding the Line

12

There were so many sudden deaths it's hard to keep them straight. Heart attacks, accidents, suicides. A lot of suicides, and every one of them unique and unfathomable. One man shot himself—whether in frustration or exhaustion—after his building renos failed inspection. A woman killed herself over the collapse of a five-week-long Internet affair.

A man I'll call Leonard left a note for the woman who owned the house in which he rented a small apartment. In exchange for low rent, he'd been doing some work around the new house. The note, pinned to the dryer, read "The devil must die today." It indicated he was in the shed, a small enclosure attached to their carport. The homeowner didn't go to the shed. Instead, she called 9-1-1.

When we queried his name, we saw Leonard had a troubled history and that he possessed firearms.

In a case like this, you have to be prepared for every possible outcome. We had no way of knowing if he was alive or dead, if he meant to harm someone else, or if he was suicidal but, unable to kill himself, would opt to aim a gun at us and force us to shoot. They call that "suicide by cop."

For all we knew, he wasn't in there at all. My partner and I listened, but we couldn't hear a sound. There was no response when we called out.

We had to psyche ourselves up for whatever we were about to encounter. It was getting dark. Neighbours had begun to gather on the street in front of the house, drawn by two police cars on their normally very quiet street and two uniformed cops silhouetted in the carport. For a minute, we played "No, you open the door and I'll hold the flashlight." Finally, my partner opened the shed door.

Nothing. There was nothing to see. No person or body, no weapons, no gruesome scene. As we stepped inside, the door partially closed and Leonard swung out from behind it. He had hung himself right inside the door. It was clear he'd been dead for quite a while.

We notified the dispatcher and requested she call the coroner. And then we waited, and waited, for him to arrive.

I spoke with the homeowner. She was filled with mixed emotions—shook up and terribly sad for this man whom they'd taken in and who was helping with repairs to their house. But she was angry, too, that he would choose to do this in their new home, tarnishing the family's happiness—maybe forever. She was equally outraged that he hadn't considered whether her kids might come home first and find him swinging in the shed.

I wanted to console her, to offer some guarantee that time would wipe clean this stain, but I didn't know if it could. I just wanted the coroner to hurry up.

You can make yourself crazy trying to understand everyone else's pain, trying to rationalize an irrational thing. You have to do your job, and then you have to live your own life. Waiting for the coroner, my mind was leaping ahead to the evening. I needed to get out of there. It was Ashley's birthday, and we had plans. She was counting on her mother to be there and to be *all* there. But when you're in uniform and you're in charge, you can't just say, "It's too bad about all this, but I really have to get home to my kid's birthday party."

And when you finally do get home, you can't just say, "Sorry I'm late. Here's what happened." So you stuff it all in different boxes in your head and you put the lid on tight and you hope nothing happens to open those boxes and mix all the pieces up.

MY GUN BELT WAS CAUSING pain in my lower abdomen. I couldn't figure it out. It was no heavier than it had ever been, and I was wearing it the same way, but there were shifts when I would have to come back to the office or stop at home and take it off for a while. My doctor couldn't find anything wrong.

Physical pain is, at least, obvious and easy to point to. Other things going on inside me were vague and more unsettling. For years before I started a shift, I often threw up, but now my avoidance behaviours were multiplying. On my days off, I would take any route to avoid passing the police station. I'd grown to hate just driving past that building.

And I couldn't concentrate like I used to. I would begin a report to crown counsel to lay a charge on one of my files, and paperwork that normally took about forty-five minutes now filled two hours because I had to keep taking breaks, driving around on patrol and then coming back to it only to have to leave again soon. As the nights got dark, I would get anxious just being inside my police car. I wasn't afraid of the dark, but it felt so claustrophobic. I could only stand it so long before I'd have to get out and walk around to get some fresh air. When weather permitted, I'd do my paperwork sitting on a bench. If I went down into the cellblock below street level, I made a quick escape. There were no windows down there, just cement-block walls and heavy steel doors locked tight, and that made me panic thinking about earthquakes, buildings collapsing, being trapped and unable to breathe. Pretty soon I couldn't even go into a shopping mall because I couldn't see an exit door. At night I had to open the blinds and let the streetlights shine in. If I couldn't see outside, I wouldn't sleep.

I'd also started having acute sensory experiences. The first time it happened, I was driving to the hospital to see one of my in-laws, and I noticed a house where I'd been to a very gruesome death years before. My car filled with the smell of that house, the stench of bodily waste and decay made worse by summer heat. After that, I drove a different route to the hospital.

LIKE JUST ABOUT EVERY PARENT, I sat through my share of elementary school performances. As I watched the kids sing, dance, and fool around up on that stage, I'd wonder how some of them could do it, could be so convincingly upbeat. I knew things the other parents in the audience didn't—knew things because I'd been called to some of those kids' homes on several occasions.

There was a girl whose home life was chaos. Her mother was addicted to drugs, yet her father was determined to keep the family together. His intentions were honourable, and I guess it was testament to his love for his wife, the way he tried for so long, but the cost was high for his three children. The family lived in a small two-bedroom apartment, and the oldest daughter slept on a couch in the living room. She had no bedroom, no dresser for her clothes, no place of her own, yet she showed up at school each day and tried to fit in. Nobody knew she'd been awake much of the night, anxiously awaiting her mother's return. And when Mom did make it home, it was 4 a.m. and she was in a state—drunk and high, screaming and smashing things until her husband called the police and had her removed. By then, it was time for the kids to get up and get ready for school.

When I saw that little girl up on the school stage, I couldn't help but consider how her life was one long, vicious cycle over which she had no control, even if she was good at keeping it together herself. At least, I thought, she had one stable parent she could count on.

I STOPPED WEARING MY WEDDING band after a particularly hard arrest. The suspect was malevolent and wild. As we put him in the car, he looked at my hand and noted I was married. "You probably have kids," he said, staring right into my face. Then he proceeded to tell me, graphically, what he planned to do to my daughters before he dumped their bodies.

I went home and I took my ring off, and I never put it back on. Out in the street, I wanted to be just Janet or just Constable Merlo, the two identities unattached. I never again wanted anyone I loved to be threatened by their connection to me.

NOT LONG AFTER I MET Mike, he introduced me to his sister, Winona. I liked her as immediately as I'd liked him though they couldn't have been more different on the surface. While Mike was the gruff outdoorsman type, Winona was every bit the lady. She appreciated pretty things, good manners, and chivalry, and she kept a lovely and welcoming, stylish home. She was also a barrel of fun.

My parents were so far away, and across that great distance, I didn't want to trouble them with all the difficulties in my life. In many ways, Mike and Winona filled the void; they were my family on Vancouver Island. Shortly after we became close, Mike moved south to Victoria, where he had a wonderful condo by the ocean. As often as we could, Winona and I hit the highway, making the hour-and-a-half trek to visit him. We dubbed ourselves Thelma and Louise, and the first stop was the liquor store because we planned to kick back and stay the night.

We took turns driving, though Winona complained I handled the curves like I was driving a police cruiser in hot pursuit. Every so often I noticed she was hanging on as if for dear life.

Wayne never gave me a hard time about those excursions; still I felt guilty about ditching my responsibilities and leaving my girls behind. But those getaways were important to me. In the car, Winona and I could unload on each other. She was a lone parent who worked damn hard at the Department of Fisheries, and she carried all the stress—and guilt—that came with being a working single mother. I could share my worries about Wayne and all my troubles from work, and I might end up crying, but before long Nanaimo would disappear in the rear-view mirror and we'd be laughing.

When we got to Mike's, that gruff mountain man would have his place shining, and he'd be grinning like a kid at Christmas. My favourite roast chicken would be in the oven, and we'd all pretend he hadn't just picked it up, pre-cooked, at the store.

Over a few drinks we'd spill our guts, and then I'd sleep deeply until four in the morning, when Mike would get up with Attu and I'd hear "Psssst. Coming for a walk, Shorty?" Our mornings together were a rare thing now that he lived so far outside my patrol area, so I'd drag myself out of bed and go to the beach with him and the dog. Attu would frolic off-leash like a 150-pound puppy on that dark beach, and it was the same quiet, blue dark before sunrise in which my friendship with Mike had blossomed. Wrapped inside it, I could share my blackest moments. Side by side, short and tall, we could both dare to talk about our hopes and dreams.

By the time we returned to the condo, Winona would be up and raring to go, ready to have some fun. The three of us would stroll downtown Victoria, eat barbequed pork from the Chinese deli, and meander through unique little boutiques. One store in particular always drew us in—it was full of greeting cards and gag gifts, most of them dripping with sexual innuendo. No matter how far Winona and I moved away in that store, we couldn't escape the sound of a large man giggling like a schoolgirl.

As soon as I felt like I was really starting to relax, it was time to go home. On the trip back north, Winona and I would talk about when we'd be able to get away again. Long before we got to Nanaimo, we'd be planning our sequel.

MONTHS AFTER LEONARD HUNG HIMSELF in that shed, I got a troubling call from the homeowner. I'd stopped by a few times in the weeks after his suicide just to check on the family. Now she wanted me to come over and see something that had come in the mail. It was a letter from Leonard—written and addressed to her in his handwriting but postmarked just two days earlier, in Nanaimo. In the letter, he wrote about all of the hopes and dreams he had for that year, the goals he had set, and what he hoped to have accomplished by year's end.

She was shaken and baffled. So was I.

We racked our brains, and then we both told other people, got their brains involved. Someone suggested we check in with Leonard's church, so I went to see the pastor there and told her about the letter. She became terribly upset, but she solved the mystery. It was common practice in that church's support group to begin the New Year by writing a letter to someone the writer cared about—someone inspirational. The letters were addressed, gathered, and held, and the church office mailed them out during the year. The idea was to let those important people in your life know your aspirations as the year opened, and then they'd see if you were still on track.

The pastor had performed Leonard's eulogy, but in the rush of her duties, she had completely missed pulling the letter from the stack before it was mailed.

Knowing all this just made it harder to understand his suicide. He'd done the right things—cleaned up and reached out to a church. He thought so highly of the woman who had given him shelter that he'd chosen her to receive his letter—a letter in which he laid out his plans and dreams for the future. A month later, he ended his life in her shed.

THERE WAS A LITTLE BOY in Ashley's school who was being raised by a single father. They were always seen together, father and son, inseparable. But the father died of a congenital disease, and in the absence of any family to take him in—his mother had long before left his life—the eight-year-old boy went into foster care. Not long after that, I sat in the school auditorium at my daughter's Christmas concert. A wonderful, happy concert, full of life, and then that little boy whose life had just been ripped apart began to sing. Everyone fell still and silent as his lone voice filled the auditorium with "Little Toy Trains."

Close your eyes/Listen to the skies/All is calm, all is well...

I began to cry. He would never have another Christmas with his father, probably wouldn't have a true family to celebrate Christmas with for a long time to come. But his voice never wavered. It overwhelmed me, and I could only hope the people around me couldn't see my tears or hear my stifled sobs. I was a police officer—I was supposed to keep things together. But there I was, falling apart.

Little boy, don't you think it's time you were in bed?

Saying Goodbye

13

MY FATHER-IN-LAW'S HEALTH was deteriorating quickly, and the pain I experienced when I wore my gun belt was getting worse. My doctor sent me for an ultrasound. A few days later, Jack's doctor told us Jack wasn't likely to make it much longer. His organs were shutting down. We were taking turns at the bedside, comforting each other as best we could on that terrible day, and then my doctor called. He needed to see me as soon as possible. Since his office was across the street from the hospital, I went straight over.

The ultrasound showed growths on both my ovaries as big as baseballs. It wasn't clear what they were or if they were malignant, so he wanted to operate right away. He didn't want to take any chances.

I walked back across the street in a daze. I couldn't tell Wayne, sitting there by his father's deathbed with his mom, his sister, and our daughters. This new worry I would shoulder alone for a while. I quietly gathered up the kids and took them home for dinner. Wayne and Jeannie came too, planning to grab a quick bite to eat and head back. As soon as they came through the door, the hospital called. Jack Merlo was gone.

Two weeks later, I was prepped for surgery. My doctor, the same one who'd delivered my babies and performed my hysterectomy, leaned over me and explained that the surgery would be extensive, that I'd have to be opened right up. Someone else might have bolted at that, but I needed to trust in something, so I put my faith in him.

The tumours were benign and, I suppose, a blessing—a reprieve from the impending transfer it seemed I wouldn't be able to avoid. At least while I convalesced, I had time to spend with Kay. She was devastated by the loss of her husband and seemed more fragile with each passing week. Wayne was beside himself with grief and worry.

When I returned to work in the fall, the fight began anew. During my sick leave, not a single member had been transferred into Nanaimo from a remote posting. Two female members, however, had been transferred out of our office. One was involved with a member in a detachment farther south on the island, so she was posted closer to him. The other, according to office gossip, had recently left her husband to pursue an affair with a senior ranking member in our detachment. She'd been transferred within arm's reach, about fifteen minutes away.

There was a lot of gossip going around. You could enter any office in the building and hear people talking about somebody else. It got so bad you hated to leave a room because you knew you'd be the next topic. And it wasn't just a few rumour mongers out to make malice—so many good people were frustrated and angry. It was generally believed that several people were enjoying preferential treatment with senior officers while others were getting pushed to work harder without reward. Animosity festered, and nerves were raw before a shift even began.

Late in December, I received a form with five choices for postings, all in Surrey on the mainland. I could have my pick. The form had to be signed and returned by the end of the year, so I had less than a week to think about my decision. I knew if I didn't accept one of the five, if I refused to sign the paper, I would forfeit any choice at all. The RCMP would be free to move me wherever they had an operational need—anywhere in Canada. So of course I signed it.

The RCMP has always moved its members based on operational needs. The practice remains unchanged since the days when members were all men—single men, off on a great adventure, or married men whose families would follow the breadwinner. The world changed, families evolved, and the workforce adjusted, but the RCMP's policy of moving its members like so many pawns on a chessboard stayed the same.

Of course sometimes, transfers were used to solve individual problems. In my case, they claimed I wasn't ambitious enough, that a move would be good for my career. Maybe it would get me performing up to snuff. I had a supervisor who asked me for blow jobs, and sex toys in my files. I'd been dealing with multiple health and family crises. At work, there was never time to properly process tragedy—never mind paperwork—due to chronic manpower shortages. We were out there, putting ourselves in danger on every call we took because we knew there weren't enough resources for backup. So yes, I suppose it's true I wasn't doing a stellar job by then.

The RCMP never offered me an avenue to deal with any of those issues. Instead, they suggested a transfer.

Move the problem is the RCMP way. We all knew stories of members who were alleged to have committed all manner of grievous infractions—assaults, drug offences, property crimes—who were suddenly posted to another detachment while the complaints against them were quickly swept under an impervious rug. I'd heard allegations that a member was moved after he propositioned teenage girls at a local high school. I knew of a member who had a relationship with a community police station volunteer, a young female applicant for the RCMP. When she realized he had no intention of leaving his wife, she ended it. That's when, she claimed, he savagely sexually assaulted her. I can't confirm this is what occurred, but I do know I was asked to come and look at her wounds—the bruises and the bite marks on her breasts. There was a brief investigation, after which her claims were dismissed, and he was quickly promoted and transferred. Her application to join the RCMP, meanwhile, was dismissed. I heard they'd deemed having an affair with a married man conduct not becoming for a future police officer.

The force responsible for holding others—even our government—accountable to the law has an interesting conflict of interest built right in. The RCMP investigates its own. Over a long period of time, the practice of admitting no wrong, of keeping things quiet and transferring the problem, has warped the culture of the organization. So many stories, so many secrets, were crammed under the damn rug that making any meaningful change meant risking too much exposure, too much damage to the public trust.

WAYNE KEPT THE CONCRETE FLOOR in the cellblock polished to a high gloss, and it rattled him when they brought in a sloppy drunk who peed on his floor or when hard heels left scuff marks. One night, an officer wrote a message to Wayne on the shiny cellblock floor with his black boot. That contempt for his hard work was too much for Wayne. He stormed out and came home, where he scared me as I sat at the computer. He shouted the story, or part of it, and when I didn't react just right, he screamed, "You're one of them!" and flung his heavy fistful of iron keys at me.

They missed, thank God, because they would have left a permanent dent in my head.

Kay's deteriorating physical state was fueling Wayne's erratic behaviour. On top of her illness, Kay was desperately worried about Wayne, and about whether he would be able to cope if I had to move away. She knew our family was struggling, and she believed the separation would tear us apart permanently. I did too, but I didn't tell her that.

I was getting nowhere with my pleas to Staffing. I'd even had doctors write letters explaining that I was needed at home. All my requests were rejected, my resistance met with an incredulous "But you signed the paper."

I felt like I was shouting "10-33! 10-33!" and no one was responding.

In a nearby detachment, I knew a member who was also being forced to move from his family, so I contacted him, and we agreed to switch postings. It wouldn't cost the RCMP a cent, but it would achieve the goal of getting us the hell out of where we weren't welcome. That solution was dismissed.

I wrote to my division representative, the member who was supposed to help with issues like this. I told him about my caretaker responsibilities, about the strain this transfer was putting on our marriage. In his reply, he wrote that if my marriage did fall apart, I'd have a better chance of getting the transfer reconsidered since I'd have custody issues to work around. It was absurd. He was telling me, essentially, that there was no way to save my family and that the RCMP would only care after it was ripped to shreds.

EVERY SO OFTEN, AN INCIDENT reminded me that no matter who they were, every person and every family had their problems. I had learned never to make snap judgments, never to assume that behind a successful career or a serene smile, or the locked front door of an affluent house, things were as wonderful as they seemed on the outside.

In the spring, I received a call about a group of kids having a party on the beach. I went alone, and when I arrived, the kids saw the police car and, of course, scattered. Or most of them did. Two young men were simply too drunk to flee.

When I spoke to them, it was clear they were quite intoxicated. They were also underage and had a small amount of alcohol still in their possession. I had to follow up with some sort of consequences though, under the Liquor Control and Licensing Act, I had a lot of options amid the requirements. Because they were minors, they couldn't be left with any alcohol. I could seize it, write them tickets, and preserve the alcohol as evidence for court, or I could pour it at their feet and deliver them home to their parents. I could hold them there on the beach and call their parents to come collect them, too—or, for greater impact, I could arrest them, take them to the police station, and then phone their parents. Either way, it would be an attention getter, an inconvenience in the middle of the night that ensured the parents realized the seriousness of their teenagers' drinking.

Despite being drunk, the two young men in my custody were very polite, and that definitely influenced what I did with them. Respect is a two-way street, and I always tried to give as good as I got. I decided I had time to drive them home to their parents. There was barely any alcohol left to seize anyway, and I knew their hangovers would serve as a good portion of their punishment. I told them both to get in my car.

At the front door of the first boy's house, I explained to his parents the nature of the call and the problem. I made sure to mention that their son had been courteous, so I'd decided not to issue a ticket. The parents were as respectful as their son, and they thanked me for bringing him home safe. I felt certain they'd follow through with some appropriate consequences. All was well.

I got back into my car with the other boy and started out toward his house. I had entered his name and address in my notebook, but I hadn't paid attention to his surname. As we neared his home, he became increasingly agitated, saying, "You can't take me home. My dad's gonna kill me!"

I'd heard that a hundred times before. It was typical teenager manoeuvring—it starts with "my dad will kill me" and moves on to pleading to get dropped anywhere else but at home. And why not? Nobody wants to get into trouble with their parents if they can avoid it; nobody wants to get disciplined, to be grounded. Or worse, to be a disappointment.

I had a duty to drop this young man off at his home, a responsibility to release him into the custody of his parents, and that's exactly what I intended to do. As we drove closer, his concern turned to fear, and then to outright sobbing.

Noisy bawling is not a typical teenage boy's maneuver. My gut told me there just might be something to his fear. I pulled over and turned around to see the young man curled up in the fetal position in the backseat, crying like a baby, shaking violently. There was no way he was faking that reaction.

So I asked him to tell me about it, and I learned quite a lot about that young man in a short time. Through his tears, he told me of the high expectations his parents had for him, the enormous pressure he was under to succeed, the punishment for failure. He told me about physical abuse, the beatings his father laid on him, his fear of angering a man who, from the sound of it, had some terrible issues with anger.

I asked the boy if he'd ever talked to anybody about what was going on in his house. He hadn't, because, he said, nobody would ever believe him. And if he told someone at school and the counsellor got wind of it, they would have to involve the

Ministry of Children and Families—but to what end? Even if an investigation was launched, no one would take his word over his parents' word, and then life at home would be much worse because he had dared to speak up.

Although this kid was terrified to disclose, he'd obviously given it a lot of thought. He was able to outline for me each probable outcome for every direction he might take. He begged me not to get involved.

I weighed my responsibility and wondered if I could live with myself if I laid a complaint with the ministry and later got a call telling me he'd been returned to his home and then beaten black and blue by his dad. Besides, he had an escape plan—he was just a few months from his high-school graduation and then off to university. I decided to trust his judgement and stay out of it.

We came to an agreement about what would happen next. I agreed to park a few houses away and allow him to walk home. If he got caught coming in, he would have to deal with the consequences, but I wouldn't wake his parents. I wasn't willing to make things worse for him. I did, however, need some proof that he'd actually gone into the house and hadn't slipped off into the bushes. He pointed out his bedroom window—upstairs on the front of the house—and I told him to turn the light on and off a couple of times when he got there, just to let me know he was okay.

You could argue I covered for him that night, failed in my duty as an officer of the law, but I was willing to do that based on the boy's intense fear of his father. I could get in a whole lot of trouble if my gut feeling was wrong, but it was a risk I was willing to take. Years of experience had me convinced he was telling the truth, and if he was, I had no doubt the system would never work for this kid. I'd seen enough to know the system worked to cover up crimes when important careers and reputations were at stake. The best I could do for that boy was give him my card and tell him to call me if I could ever help.

While I waited for that flicker of light, I wondered if I'd done the right thing, and I thought about how different this story would have been if the kid's father was a regular guy in a lesser neighbourhood. I would have reported what I'd been told, and if an investigation revealed violence, steps would be taken, changes made. But that night, after I saw the light in the upstairs bedroom window, I drove slowly away down one of the most affluent streets in the city. Away from the big, beautiful house of one of the city's prestigious lawyers, a man whose terrified son I never heard from again.

I SPOKE TO A MEMBERS' assistance person about the transfer, told him how exhausted I was, how I felt the RCMP's insistence I move at this point in my life felt like a violation of my rights and all that was decent. He assured me the RCMP Act allowed all kinds of civil and human rights violations. But staffing had—informally, at least—granted me a small reprieve. They were willing to delay my move until my mother-in-law passed away.

After that, every few weeks I would get a call or an email from a staffing officer, asking me how things were going. Finally I got fed up with the "Is she dead yet?" line of enquiry and told her to stop contacting me. I promised to notify her as soon as Kay took her last breath. The staffing officer wasn't impressed. She wanted me to know she'd been asking about me, not my mother-in-law.

And maybe she had been. I was too strung out to even consider that someone in the RCMP had any concern for my welfare.

THE WOMAN WAS CLEARLY STILL terrified when I arrived.

She'd simply reached over to pick up the TV remote, she explained. She wanted to change the channel, but her husband had jolted up, reached under the couch, pulled out an axe, and chased her through their big house with it.

He hadn't always been prone to violent attacks, but this one hadn't come out of the clear blue either. For a long time, she said, her husband had been growing more and more paranoid. In recent years, this had escalated until he believed the world and now his wife, too, were out to get him. He had taken to hiding knives, hatchets, and meat cleavers all around their house, and his threats had become an almost daily facet of her life.

Almost daily, yet she'd gone on living with his bizarre behaviour and had never spoken to anyone about it. She couldn't. She knew she would be the one who was deemed crazy—her husband was a well-respected health professional and together they had a wonderful reputation in the community. But behind the closed doors of their beautiful home, she lay in bed terrified every night that in his paranoid state he'd stab her while she slept. Until the night he actually came after her with an axe, however, she had maintained her silence, fearing that, given her husband's prestigious public image, no one would believe her.

That woman's house, the lawyer's house, my house—three out of so many where secret dramas were playing out behind drawn curtains and locked doors, each so different yet joined together in a deafening silence.

Our stories were very different, but I understand why that woman kept quiet, how it happens. I'd also allowed the slow creep of mental illness to turn my house into a frightening fortress. By this time, Wayne was wrapping our remote controls in cellophane so they didn't get fingerprints on them. I couldn't tell anyone that, of course. It sounded as dubious as a psychiatrist hiding weapons around his house, or as unlikely as a group of high ranking officers in the RCMP driving their subordinates to the brink of despair with harassment and callous disrespect.

Partly I went along because it was so gradual and I was so

stressed, so distracted by everything else, that I didn't realize how bad it was getting. Partly, I still hoped Wayne's increasingly bizarre behaviour would disappear when things settled down. Mostly, I think, I was afraid of everything blowing apart if I didn't go along.

Silence never really solves anything. Eventually, the lid blows off or someone tears down the facade to expose what's really happening. It's usually someone who feels backed into a corner, so scared or angry or desperate that they're willing to risk whatever terrible price they'll have to pay.

The river that ran through Nanaimo was swollen with spring runoff. I loved to park near that river at night and sit on a bench while I did my paperwork, listening to the rushing water. It was like thunder, like waves on the beach—a welcome kind of mindless sound that drowned out the racket in my head. But one night, as I sat there working, something besides white noise and paperwork edged in. The river was raging, and I started to think about all that water, about the weight of my gun belt, my boots, and my bulletproof vest. The water was deep and tumultuous, but surely all the weight of the equipment I wore would be enough to hold me under until eventually whatever was left of me surfaced in the harbour.

It seemed like such an easy way to end all the problems I couldn't seem to solve. Kay was spending more and more time in the hospital, and we knew she was nearing the end. Wayne was giving in more and more to his anguish. The work I'd believed in as if it were my true religion now seemed overwhelming and pointless. And now the organization I had joined with so much pride was making me choose between it and my family.

One jump and I'd be carried away, done with it all.

But almost immediately, I thought about my daughters. No amount of despair was worth leaving them and missing the rest of their lives—the driving lessons, the graduations, the heartaches and weddings, and even the grandchildren that were out there beyond what I could see.

I stood up, gathered up my things quickly, turned my back on that raging water, and drove away fast from my easy way out on the river.

A handful of days later, I blew up at the end of a dayshift in the general duty section of the office. I'm not even sure what triggered it. I was tired and overwhelmed, and then I was shouting and crying. I went to the change room, put my uniform and gun belt in my locker, and I left. That last part was important—there was still a sane piece inside of me that knew if I didn't get out of there, I might do something stupid.

I went to my doctor the next day and told her about all the stress, the weird panic attacks and crazy thoughts I'd been having. I told her about the river. She recommended I take a break, and we agreed I couldn't be much good to the public in my current state. The doctor wrote me a medical letter so I could take time off work until my life back got back on track.

A few weeks later, Kay was hospitalized for the last time. She told us she kept waking at night to see Jack standing at the foot of her hospital bed. He'd say, "Kay, it's time. The kids will be fine." But she didn't want to leave her kids, so she continued to hang on, her lungs filling with more and more fluid.

Finally, she slipped into a deep sleep. On the day we suspected might be her last, Wayne, Jeannie, and I stayed at the hospital. Wayne had gone for coffee with a friend of his who'd stopped by, and Jeannie went to speak with the nurses. I took advantage of my time alone with Kay to tell her how much I loved her and how blessed I felt to have such a wonderful mother-in-law. I knew over the years she had loved me and that made it a little easier to live so far away from my own mother. As I held her hand, I assured her I would raise her granddaughters with every ounce of respect and kindness I could muster. I also promised her I would do my best to love and support her son. And then I told her it was okay to go with Jack.

Jeannie came back into the room, and we both saw just a single tear slip from Kay's right eye. She hadn't responded to conversation for days, but I know she could hear us. When Wayne checked back in at the room, we told him her breaths were getting further and further apart. He loved his mother so much and losing her was so painful that he just couldn't be in the room when she passed, so he went out to wait. Jeannie and I held her hands as she finally let go.

Watching Kathleen Merlo take her last breath, I had a profound revelation. At the end, on your deathbed, it's family who are there for you. Not your co-workers, your bosses, or the human resources people. Just your family. That's what has to matter most.

Losing the Light

14

MONTHS INTO MY STRESS LEAVE, I was still struggling to get my head on straight. One day walking to the store, I ran into Wayne's cousin, a woman I'd known for fifteen years and saw about three times a week. We stopped and had a brief conversation about our families. The whole time, I was desperately trying to remember her name.

And on top of dealing with my grieving family and helping with Kay's estate, I wasn't sleeping well. I was lying awake, ruminating on one problem or another for hours. When I finally did fall asleep, I fell into a world of horrible nightmares.

ACCORDING TO RCMP POLICY, MEMBERS who are off work for more than a month—whether on holidays or on medical leave—are expected to turn in their guns for safekeeping. Mine was safely stowed in my locker at work. I knew the policy, but I also knew it wasn't really enforced. I'd taken two maternity leaves and two long sick leaves in my career, and no one had ever requested my gun.

Still, I talked it over with the corporal on my watch, and he said not to worry about it. He promised to pop by some evening and pick up the key for my locker. I guess he forgot, and later, he went on an extended holiday, which I knew nothing about. No one else contacted me. I suppose maybe they called. As shift workers, Wayne and I had an above-average aversion to telemarketers, so we never answered calls from unknown numbers. But no one at the RCMP ever left a phone message about my gun. No one ever mentioned it to Wayne at work, either; if I'd known it was a big deal, I could have sent the key with him.

In August, a priority envelope arrived from the police station. Inside was a letter from the officer in charge, telling me I was in breach of my responsibilities while on long-term leave. He said, "It is my understanding that your situation has deteriorated to the point that you feel no obligation to comply with the requirements of your employment. You are reminded of your commitment to the RCMP and the community in which you serve." It went on for pages about those requirements, but what it all boiled down to was I had failed to hand over my gun. The letter contended the detachment was having "difficulty" getting in touch with me, so finally, they'd had to cut the lock off my locker to retrieve my weapon. If I wanted the new key, I'd have to get it from my watch commander.

The letter ended with an offering of sincere condolences for the "significant loss to my family."

IN THE SUMMER OF 2007, a civilian, William Elliott, was named the RCMP's new commissioner. A number of scandals had rocked the organization, and his appointment was touted as a fresh start, a chance to clean things up. Thank God, I thought, an outsider, somebody who wasn't already chest-deep in the old boys' club—somebody objective who could make some real changes.

I was looking forward to a new style of leadership. After all, I knew first-hand the effects of the old system. I had suffered bullying, harassment, and the callous disregard of management. I had seen preferential treatment supplant fairness, and I had endured a staggering lack of compassion that destroyed my mental health and almost tore my family apart. Like the woman whose husband had pulled an axe out from under the couch, I was finally desperate enough to blurt out everything and beg for help.

On September 16, 2007, I wrote a long letter to the new commissioner. I knew it contravened policy to go over so many heads, but I didn't care. I really did want to congratulate him, to offer my support, and to wish him well in his very challenging new position. But I also wanted him to see what was going on, how issues surrounding transfers were damaging families, how uneven treatment of members eroded trust. I told him how members who chose to leave their marriages were allowed to stay close by for custody reasons while I was punished for staying in a two-income, no-mortgage family.

I acknowledged that while I had signed up for a career that came with the possibility of being posted anywhere in the country, he could surely understand how life changes, how people get settled over sixteen years. I reminded him how one of the RCMP's issues was that it was losing good people to local police forces because they wanted to stay put.

"I am an old fashioned girl with an old fashioned commitment to my marriage and children," I wrote. "I love the first line general duty policing and love the public I work with. I don't want to have to make the choice to leave it."

Over five pages, I explained that although I'd been called a "fucking woman with a big mouth" during my career, I actually didn't want to cause trouble. To illustrate that point, I devoted about six sentences to the sexual harassment I had suffered in silence.

I ended the letter with "Hopefully you can do something to help my family. I would be eternally grateful."

I sent the letter express mail so it would get to Commissioner Elliott directly, and waited for his reply. More than a month passed before I received a letter from Stockwell Day, then the Minister of Public Safety, thanking me for my correspondence and telling me a copy of it would be sent to Mr. Elliott.

That delay was infuriating, but I still felt confident I would hear from Elliott and that things were going to get better. In fact, I never heard directly from him at all—and things got much worse.

Wayne's obsessive compulsive tendencies were taking a toll on all of us. The girls couldn't shower long enough to rinse the conditioner out of their hair without him banging on the bathroom door like he was going to come through it.

When he'd go to work, I snuck out with the girls to do normal things. We would shop for household items, and I'd pray that he hadn't taken an odometer reading before he'd gone to work. It was all very cloak and dagger, and I would swear the girls to secrecy. I'm not proud of that, how I entangled them in my lies to their father. I'm not proud either of how, before he came home, we tore around the house like crazy people, tidying, straightening, hiding any evidence of a daytrip. I remember concealing cardboard packaging in the basement and sneaking it out on recycling day. I knew I was enabling him, but I also knew I had to save my children from enduring his wrath and an endless string of tirades and ugly arguments.

I'D MADE A PROMISE TO Kay that I would be the best mother and wife I could, so I began to see a psychiatrist, hoping that would help get me back on track. After some discussion, it was easy for him to diagnose why everything had become so grey and jumbled in my head. I was pretty textbook. I was suffering from Post Traumatic Stress Disorder, or PTSD, a debilitating anxiety disorder. PTSD can be triggered by a traumatic experience or brought on by long-term exposure to chronic high-stress situations. It's not clear why some people develop it while others exposed to the same incidents do not, but it is known to affect a lot of police officers and other emergency responders. That's not surprising to me given the constant anxiety the job created every day—the gruesome and the heartbreaking, the devastating sense of being overwhelmed with no end in sight. In my case, the harassment dealt by co-workers and the terrible pressure of being told I would have to move far away from my children intensified all of the unavoidable difficulties of the job. My mental circuits had overloaded, and I lost the ability to compartmentalize. I couldn't escape the memories; instead I relived the worst scenes in a hundred variations. I had flashbacks, nightmares, and irrational panic reactions to ordinary events. I was constantly anxious. I couldn't step down from a state of high alert.

PTSD is not a new phenomenon. Over the years it has had different names—soldiers returning from wars were once dubbed "shell shocked." But for police officers—for me—the battlefield wasn't some far-off location I'd come home from. It was all around me, every day. Like all police officers, I lived in the shadow of the horrible things I had seen.

When the driver lost control in that torrential rainfall and struck the concrete median that separated the northbound from southbound lanes, the car cracked the concrete and sheared off a big chunk of it. The damage was very noticeable, but not bad enough to warrant replacing the median. Every time I drove southbound on that highway during the day, I saw that gouge in the concrete and remembered the accident and the awful aftermath. Every time I drove by there at night, especially when it was raining, I relived the scene as if it were happening right then, all over again. And then I'd go home knowing that when I went to bed, I would dream I was back there, and I would hear that death rattle. And sometimes it would be the same exact scene, but when I looked into the car, it was one of my girls in there, twisted and injured and dying, except I could see her face as plain as day.

I would wake up terrified, gasping, unable to shake the image of my daughter's dying face inside that car.

ERIN WAS GETTING READY TO go out trick or treating with her friends for Halloween when I remembered that my flashlight—the fantastic Maglite I'd bought on Salt Spring Island when Wayne and I were dating—was in my locker at work. I contacted my watch commander, asking if he'd leave the new locker key for Wayne so he could grab the flashlight. The watch commander let me know he'd given the key to the staff sergeant in charge of operations. I called the staff sergeant, and he said no. He didn't think that was good enough. If I wanted the key, he insisted, I first had to come talk to him.

Very recently, the psychiatrist I was seeing had received a letter from the RCMP Health Services questioning his medical diagnosis and suggesting he was helping a disgruntled employee play the system. He was at the top of his field, well respected and not happy at all to have his diagnostic abilities called into question. Under the circumstances, I was reluctant to go into the office.

I reminded the staff sergeant I was off on medical leave and told him I didn't feel strong enough to see him. He pushed hard though, refusing to give in, talking about duty and commitment and shaming me until I agreed.

All I wanted was that flashlight, but he insisted we have a chat first. He interrogated me about my medical condition, forcing me to explain things about my personal life and my mental state—things I didn't really understand myself yet—and about the depression I was suffering due to the hormonal changes that instant menopause brings. I sat in his office crying and broken, humiliated. He had no right to all this. I had a doctor and he had filed the requisite paperwork with the RCMP. My doctor was accountable to Health Services, and I was entitled to confidentiality.

In hindsight, I wish I'd just gone in there with bolt cutters and retrieved my personal things.

The staff sergeant even tried offering me an open highway patrol position, which would be considered a transfer. If they gave me that position, would I come back to work? I guess he thought I'd go for it and the ruse would be up. I told him, again, that I was unable to come back to work until I was cleared by my doctors.

When I finally lit into him, telling him how the favouritism, the double standards, and the sexual harassment had taken a toll on me, he said, "Janet, you have to leave the past behind.... So you found a dildo in your drawer and had a bit of a hard time, who cares? Put it behind you and move on."

I left his office that day just as I expected: crying, upset, humiliated, and beaten down. I suppose I had the right to refuse to see him and tell him my medical issues were personal, but the RCMP doesn't work that way. Had I refused to talk, that would have given them more ammunition to spread rumors that I was playing the system. He told me that day that he wanted me to come in to his office every two weeks to see him and give him an update on my progress.

I agreed to give him regular updates, but I was lying. I just wanted my key.

When questioned later about this visit, the staff sergeant said he was simply complying with RCMP policy to stay in touch with those off on long-term sick leave to see how they were doing.

I had to leave his office and walk through the whole building to get to my locker, terrified of what I might encounter around every corner. I got my flashlight and fled. It was just one more time I had to run from that building with red swollen eyes, biting back sobs and sick to my stomach.

It was months before I worked up the courage to go back there and get the rest of my personal things. When I did, I discovered that my locker had been cleared out and given to another member. My things were put in a box in storage—but not all my things. They'd been looted, and anything worth taking was gone, including a sweater my grandmother had knit for me and the very expensive nylon gun belt I'd bought myself because the regulation leather was too stiff against my hysterectomy scar. Several of my police notebooks were also gone. Those notebooks contained information germane to undecided cases. It was illegal to throw them away and whoever took them knew, if I was called into court on anything contained in those notebooks, I would be humiliated on the stand.

Another symptom of PTSD is a kind of emotional avoidance and detachment. It's the flipside of the hypervigilance and sensory overload, a numbness that serves to help you avoid triggers the way swelling around an injured joint helps buffer the pain and protect the tissue. I'd lost interest in doing the things I used to find so enjoyable. I couldn't complete a craft. I wanted to make a cross-stitch picture for my mother, as I'd done in the past, but before I was even half done I'd move on to another project and then another. I abandoned them all, shoving them in the closet by the front door until it was full of clutter. The fact that I no longer had any homemade gifts to give away troubled me, but not enough to inspire me to get something finished.

I DIDN'T GET A RESPONSE from Commissioner Elliott. His office didn't intervene to help with my transfer problems or even acknowledge them. What happened instead is that the RCMP asked me to give a statement about my allegations of sexual harassment. I knew there was little I could do but comply, and I was aware that once I made a statement about the harassment, my career was over. Though rationally I knew I had nothing left to lose, I was afraid—terrified of the inevitable backlash—and it took me months to work up the courage and mental concentration to do it.

According to the RCMP Act, it's an offence for a member to speak out about the organization, so I had to ensure I was protected. I certainly didn't want to be railroaded into some new mess because I'd become a whistleblower. There was a lawyer in Calgary who was experienced in RCMP matters. She'd been retained by other members who had successfully sued the force, so I sought her legal advice. We went through years of notes, emails, and messages before I submitted my statement. I paid for all of this out of my pocket—the flights and hotels in Calgary, the hourly wages for the lawyer. The process cost my family thousands of dollars.

The following summer, the member leading the investigation wanted to meet with me, but I wouldn't see him alone. Initially he too had told me to put these things behind me and move on. I insisted we meet in the presence of my lawyer, and I flew to Calgary. During the interview, I realized the whole process was for nothing. The investigator told me that none of the members named in my statement—neither perpetrators nor bystanders—could recall any of the incidents I mentioned. He suggested that what I had experienced were nothing more than individual personality conflicts.

I asked the investigator point blank, "You have been in this outfit for twenty-five years. Do you mean to tell me that, in all that time, you never witnessed any harassment of females in the force? Can you look me in the eye right here, right now, and tell me you have never seen it?"

He looked at me and said, "This interview is about you, not about me."

I thanked him for that answer. His deflection confirmed for me that he was well aware of the harassment issues. It also confirmed that I might as well have spent my time smashing my head against a wall. Still, I held on to a glimmer of faith, however naive, that when the results reached Ottawa, someone would see inconsistencies in the investigation. Surely someone would be held accountable for something.

For years, bath time had been a respite after hard, busy days. I would light candles, read a book, and finally relax. It was a small oasis of peace, an important one, and it was one of the last things to leave me. Now, when I tried to relax in the tub, my anxiety took over, my mind running wild with apprehension. If I left Wayne, how would I provide for the girls? Would Wayne snap and hurt me? Could I pay the bills this month? Was the RCMP going to destroy me? On and on it swirled.

Bedtime was another trial, another chance to torment myself while I waited for sleep to come. I'd tried sleeping aids, but they left me so groggy the next day I couldn't do anything, so instead I just tried to push myself to the point of exhaustion before I climbed into bed.

My dreams were worse than my waking thoughts. I dreamt that I was drowning, swept away in a big wave at Tofino. I dreamt that the burnt bodies in a house I'd seen once were my friends. I could smell the smoke. I could see their charred remains. Over and over, I dreamt the rain and the dark and the silence, the beam of my flashlight, two strangers suspended in the wreckage morphing into my parents or my daughters. Night after night, I woke up frantic and went to check on my girls, to make sure they were sleeping in their beds.

So many nights, unable to sleep, I would go sit by the fireplace and stare into the flames.

Fighting for My Life

15

Winona and I shared a birthday, so every year Mike planned a joint party for us; in 2008, it was a barbeque at our friend Tony's. But something was up with Mike that night. He grew increasingly agitated as the evening wore on, and he had a few more drinks than normal. In the years I'd known him, I'd never seen this side of him.

Winona was the designated driver, and Mike was supposed to stay at Tony's, but as we were leaving, he announced he was coming back to Winona's house. He asked me to drive with him. Concerned that he'd had too much to drink, I told him to come with us and leave his vehicle behind. He insisted I come with him instead. When I refused, he got mad and sped off. He made it safely to Winona's house, but I was angry that he'd endangered himself and others, angry that he'd put me in that position. We didn't talk about it again. I never asked what was so important that he needed me to come along as his passenger.

Over the next several weeks, I didn't chat much with Mike, but Winona told me he wasn't feeling well. Then, in late

November, Mike let us know he had cancer. Very soon, he was admitted to hospital; the prognosis was not good. On December 30, I was struck by an overwhelming need to drive to Victoria and see him. I called Winona, and we arranged to leave the next day.

We found Mike in the ICU. He was groggy, but he knew us, and he smiled. The nurses explained there was nothing they could do for him; they were in the process of moving him to a regular room until they could find a bed in a hospice centre, in palliative care.

Through heavy medication, Mike complained of being too hot, so we asked the nurses for a fan. Winona set it up at the edge of his bed. We told Mike if it didn't cool him down, we'd have to fly him to Hawaii where sexy girls with palm branches could fan him. That brought a grin and a thumbs-up. Then we struggled to help him sit up where he could feel the breeze. After a few minutes on the edge of the bed, Mike fell backwards and took his last breath.

Winona ran for the nurses, but it was too late. Just like that, his big heart had stopped beating and I lost a best friend and a big brother.

In the spring, Winona's nephew arranged for us to spread Mike's ashes atop a nearby mountain—the highest one we could climb without someone getting hurt. That's what Mike had wanted. Along with Winona's sister, brother-in-law, and nephew, we rode quads up Mount Benson. It was a beautiful, sunny day, but underneath us the road was muck. More than once we got stuck in the mud and had to spin our way out. By the time we got to the top, we had mud in our teeth, but it was worth it to see sophisticated Winona whizzing along on that quad, thoroughly splattered and loving every minute of it, her smile radiant. Mike would have been so proud.

On that mountain, we set Mike free, watched him soar like a thousand shooting stars.

WITH THE STRESS OF LOOKING after and worrying about Kay and Jack gone from our lives, I had hoped Wayne would relax a little and his mental state would begin to improve. Instead, he seemed to get worse. He plunged into a deep depression and became increasingly prone to fits of rage. If I tried to talk to him about it, he'd fly off the handle, call me a "fucking fat cow" or something equally nasty. I was in my own deep hole, and those insults started to sound right to my ears.

I was worried about Ashley, though. She heard her share of insults, too, and Wayne was so hard on her, his expectations so high. He acted as if, at fifteen, she should be fully grown up. Her spirit was taking a beating. I could see how nervous she became when her father was around. Ashley had eczema, and when Wayne came home from work, she would scratch her arms constantly, sometimes making them bleed.

Maybe there was still some latent Catholic obedience in me that made even this seem less of a sin than leaving my husband.

I'm not trying to paint myself as the martyr or deny that I didn't sometimes lose it, too. I snapped, I yelled, I sometimes took my stress out on the girls when I should have found another outlet. But it wasn't a regular thing, a constant attack. I always apologized, and I always meant it.

But as stressful as home was, the outside world was worse. I was afraid to leave the house because the men I'd named in my statement as problems within the RCMP were out there. They shopped at that mall, went to the cinema, ate in the restaurants in Nanaimo. I didn't know what the punishment might be for speaking out against them, and I didn't want to find out. When I walked our dog, I left the house wearing a baseball cap in case a police car passed me along the way. I never stopped at a coffee shop with a marked car in the parking lot, and if I did go somewhere to eat, I sat in the back corner, slunk down and scared I'd be spotted.

The only place I felt safe, really, was in a kayak in the middle of a lake, and that just wasn't a practical solution.

While I had the luxury, at least, of hiding out at home, Wayne had to go into the police station for work. Since I'd laid my complaint, some of the RCMP members kept dropping comments into their conversations with him—not direct rebukes about being married to a rat, but sideways remarks about how easy it would be for them to get rid of a municipal employee. All they would have to do is pull his security clearance and he'd be unable to work in the building. It made him nervous, afraid they would nab him one day leaving work with a pen in his pocket and charge him with internal theft. He was tortured by the anticipation of whatever punishment they had in store for him because I'd spoken out.

Wayne had always demonstrated such integrity, and he had no part in my fight, but that didn't matter to them; we were linked by marriage, so he was guilty, too.

AFTER KAY'S DEATH, IT FELL to Jeannie and me to figure out what to do with the house and all its contents. We'd cleaned out the perishables and the personal items, of course, but most of the stuff was too good to just discard.

Nearby, bad wiring in a grow-op had started a fire. The fire jumped to a neighbour's place and burned it to the ground, leaving an older woman homeless. Jeannie and I stopped by one afternoon to ask her family if she might need some of Kay's old things. They said what she really needed was a roof over her head. We were more than happy to help with that. For months while her insurance settlement rebuilt the woman's home, she lived in the little house on Duke Street. When she was able to return home, the house again sat empty.

I was on my way over to check on that house when an acquaintance came out to ask me where our girls had gone to daycare. Her maternity leave was almost over, and she was having trouble finding a spot for her baby. She knew I was off on medical leave, and in the course of our conversation, she asked what we were going to do with Jack and Kay's empty house. I told her we hadn't decided yet, and she suggested, almost as an aside, that I forget about returning to the RCMP and open a daycare.

Over the next few weeks, her idea kept looping around in my head. A daycare was an intriguing idea. After all, I couldn't stay on sick leave forever, though my mental health was nowhere near healthy enough to go back out on duty. Besides, now that I'd officially spoken out, my career was as good as over. And I loved being with little kids. Looking after a few might help keep my mind off all the turmoil that kicked up as soon as my thoughts were idle. I was seeing a psychologist now who was a wonderful support. She agreed this was a good idea.

With everything cleared out, the little house was perfect for a small daycare. I started with just two small children—including the baby that belonged to the neighbour who had sparked the idea. My friend Veronica helped me on days when I needed it. She was a real asset, and the number of kids in our care grew. The venture gave me somewhere to go, gave my waking hours a sense of purpose I'd been missing, and they were, for the first time in a long time, happy hours.

At first, I always went home at night, but when I couldn't take the strain with Wayne anymore, I began to use "kids coming early in the morning" as an excuse to stay overnight at the little house.

It meant leaving the girls there, and I know they missed having me at home—they would call sometimes at night, and I felt terrible about not being there. I felt afraid too, and I wouldn't sleep in the bedroom off to the side of the house because there wasn't an exit nearby. I hung a hammock near the house's centre, so I could escape through one door if Wayne or someone else tried to come through the other. That's the kind of state I was in, and I knew the best thing I could do for all of us was take a little breathing room and sort out in my head whether to end my marriage. At least we all got a respite from the constant angry battle that my marriage had become.

WINONA HAD JUST RETURNED FROM an Alaskan cruise, and I was anxious to hear all about it and see her pictures. We planned to meet at a local coffee shop. I needed some time catching up and unwinding. But at the last minute, Wayne announced he was coming with me.

He'd gotten in the habit of asking—about forty times a day—if I still loved him or, worse, insisting that I didn't. I kept saying, "Of course I love you." And I did, even if I didn't like him much of the time. He must have sensed my disappointment that he was coming along when I so needed a break from him because, on the walk over to the coffee shop, he talked about how he didn't think I loved him anymore. I tried to explain that I just wanted to visit with Winona, but he didn't let up. We were almost at the coffee shop when he started yelling, cursing, and calling me names. I was mortified for both of us. This was, after all, our neighbourhood, and everyone knew us. Wayne stood in our local 7-Eleven parking lot shouting that I was a "fucking bitch." I just kept walking, concentrating on putting one foot in front of the other. When he turned to go home, I was relieved.

Winona had grabbed a table, and I went to the counter to get my coffee. When I turned, I saw Wayne sitting with her. He'd had a change of heart.

For the next two hours, he didn't talk to me, didn't make eye contact or pass me the pictures Winona handed to him of her trip. Instead, he glanced and then laid them on the table. He wasn't the least bit interested in Alaska—he just wanted to make sure I didn't have a chance to tell her how he'd acted on the way over. I know Winona sensed the tension, but she did her best to act gracious while I did my best to smile convincingly.

For two years, I'd been waiting for RCMP Commissioner William Elliott to respond to my letter. For almost as long, I'd waited for the results of the investigation that the RCMP themselves initiated by demanding I make a statement about sexual harassment. In August 2009, I wrote William Elliott again.

Very quickly, I received a letter back from the deputy commissioner—but not to acknowledge receipt of the letter I'd just sent. Rather, this was an acknowledgement of the one I'd sent in 2007. It said, in part, "As you are aware the RCMP does not take these allegations lightly and, in fact, has an obligation to provide a harassment free environment for all of our employees."

I remember thinking how embarrassed I would be to write and sign a letter acknowledging receipt of someone's correspondence from twenty-five months earlier.

Ashley had her first boyfriend. Sam was a wonderful young man, and his amazing parents made her very welcome in their home. She spent a lot of time there and would tell me about baking cookies with Sam's mom. It broke my heart—we didn't bake at home anymore or do crafts or anything else that might make a mess and throw Wayne into a tantrum. And even with all we'd stopped doing, the stress level at our house remained through the roof.

She had her first job, too, at a fish-and-chips shack, and she saved her money all summer to buy an iPod. On a rare sunny, dry day when Wayne drove his truck, she went with him on an outing. They stopped by the house briefly to change—they were going right back out—and she left that iPod on the truck's front seat. They lingered much longer in the house than they'd planned, and when Ashley went to retrieve her iPod, it was gone.

She was devastated. The device cost a lot of money for a kid, and of course she had loaded it with all her music. Wayne was unsympathetic. He berated her for being so irresponsible, tore a strip off her for not looking after her possessions. This was such a different Wayne from the one the public knew. Out in public he was charming and given to acts of kindness, but his generous spirit never seemed to make it home with him anymore.

Ashley picked herself back up and went back to work, saved up again, and bought herself another iPod. I was so proud of her resilience.

One day when I was feeling around the seat in the truck, looking for something or other, I found the first iPod. It had been tucked up inside the seat in a place where it could never have just slipped on its own. I was furious with Wayne, but he maintained that it had taught her a lesson about taking care of things—a lesson he hadn't thought to discuss with her mother. It was as if it was him against the three of us.

Sometime later, the second iPod disappeared. Ashley was certain she'd left it on the floor of the bathroom when she'd run out to get to school in the morning, but Wayne was certain she'd been careless with it, let it fall from her backpack. Again, she was raked across the coals for her irresponsibility. But putting laundry into Wayne's overstuffed sock drawer a few weeks later, I moved a pair of socks and felt the iPod tucked in between the folds.

I confronted him in front of Ashley, told him he was being cruel and that his behaviour was out of bounds for a parent. He lost it, shouting and swearing at both of us. He called Ashley a "fucking little bitch," and not for the first time.

When I went to check on her in her bedroom, I found her

packing her bags. She was unapologetic and resolved. She wasn't blindly running away—she'd already talked to Sam's mother, who had offered Ashley a place to live where she wouldn't be yelled at and called abusive names.

I understood. She had reached her limit, and I couldn't blame her. She was showing more courage than I'd been able to muster. And as much as I admired Sam's mom for offering safe haven to my fifteen-year-old daughter, I couldn't let that be the answer. I needed to provide that home for her.

Deciding to leave someone so angry and bitter—someone in such a deep level of grief—was not easy, but Ashley's pain was a wake-up call. I had to make a change. I didn't want my girls growing up thinking a relationship with a man meant putting up and shutting up, meant trying to calm him down while he called you ugly names.

I hoped someday their relationship with their father would heal—that over time, his great love for them would win out. But I had to get them out of there.

I went home to Newfoundland for a visit and broke the news to my parents that Wayne and I were separating. I felt like a girl again, disappointing them with the spectre of divorce—though I wasn't telling them, or Wayne, or even myself that this was a permanent separation. Over the years, distance had taken a toll on my relationship with my family. We had missed out on so much shared time. I had virtually no contact with my brothers, and my relationship with my parents lacked the easy intimacy of proximity and daily details. We were far apart, so to keep them from worrying helplessly, I'd never let on just how awful my marriage had become. They must have sensed it because they were tremendously supportive. I went back to Nanaimo feeling stronger, and I convinced Wayne that we needed to sell the little house and buy a bigger one where the girls and I could live, at least until we were ready to reconcile.

He wasn't happy about it at first. He accused me of leaving him just because he was tidy and I wanted to live in filth and chaos, but he came around to the idea. At least, he said, no one would be around to mess up his things.

In November of 2009, after seventeen years of marriage, we officially separated. Ashley, Erin, and I moved into a house big enough to let us breathe deeply and relax.

IN JANUARY 2010, I WROTE to RCMP member Vaz Kassam, who I understood was looking into sexual harassment allegations. I'd learned he was contacting those involved in the investigation for an update. I was looking for answers, but by February 4, 2010, after no response came from Kassam, I decided to send yet another email—this one to British Columbia's Minister of Public Safety and Solicitor General, Kash Heed. I begged him to help me, told him my family and I had been caught in a terrible limbo for two years waiting for the RCMP to conclude an investigation into its own members. I regurgitated my story *again*, trying this time to stick to one page. I was desperate for some kind of resolution. I commended him on the stand he was taking regarding the RCMP, and I sent the email. But he never responded either.

The only communication I'd had during that two-year period was a brief meeting with the investigator initially assigned to my complaint. He met me at a restaurant in Nanaimo and asked me why I didn't just put the harassment behind me. It was virtually the same reaction I'd had from a supervisor some years before. And perhaps I could have moved on if a dildo in my file drawer had been the only issue, but there was such an accumulation of incidents, so much evidence of professional misconduct, favouritism, and rampant sexism. And layered over that was the force's lack of compassion and care for an officer in distress, its failure to listen or communicate openly, its insistence on compliance instead of integrity, and its resistance to change as its workforce evolved.

I can see all this so calmly now, but at the time I was livid. The waiting riled me up, sometimes to the point of being irrational. I stand by my claims, but I'm a little embarrassed about the tone of the emails I was sending, which sound to my ears now like rants. I was desperate. But what else was I to do against the wall of silence the RCMP put up against me?

I understood that I'd broken the code. I'd gone over a superior's head to complain, and I'd said things that would mar the organization's impeccable public image. But that image was already taking a beating in the press, and it certainly wasn't the fault of those who were finally starting to speak out.

AFTER MIKE'S DEATH, MY FRIENDSHIP with Winona grew stronger. The loss took its toll on her and on me, and we clung to each other for support and to remember the good times with him. I had confided in Mike just how troubling my marriage was and shared with him my distress about work. Now that he was gone, Winona became the person I sought solace from. We'd get together over a box of Purdy's Sweet Georgia Browns and let the chocolate and caramel sweeten our moods. But life was busy and sometimes we went a week or two without talking. We both knew, if we ever needed anything, the other was only a phone call away.

Winona called me when she got the news. Breast cancer. More than everything else that had happened, her diagnosis shook my faith in a benevolent universe. First Mike, and now Winona, stricken with cancer, in such close succession. I couldn't bear to lose another close friend, and the world couldn't afford to lose someone like Winona—someone so hard working and generous, so decent, and so willing to make herself useful to the world. To me.

I started to question everything and all those questions came down to *why not me*? I had been trudging along miserably for so long, and there were days I didn't want this life I had, so why couldn't I take this terrible burden from her? I wallowed around in that for a short time, but then I thought about what the burden would do to Ashley and Erin, who needed a parent they could count on.

Winona faced her cancer with all the strength and grace I'd come to expect from her. At first, I worried that Mike's death had left her so depleted that she didn't have enough fight, but I was wrong. Even during the worst of the treatment, she always had a smile. She made jokes about her hair falling out, and every Thursday after her chemo, when she was up to it, I took her out for a drive. We'd drink tea or sit at the beach. When her immune system was too beaten down to go out in public, we stayed in and visited. In the end, she was fighting a titanic battle that only she could fight, and all I could do was show her how much I valued her.

Later, every Friday night when she felt well enough, we went to a different pub in the city for dinner. Our dinner for two became a dinner for six as more people joined in, and we became the Friday evening pub crew.

I was feeling quite down about the mess of my life in those days, but watching Winona fight for her life made one thing clear. I couldn't give up. I had to find in myself the same grace and strength that she showed.

Speaking Out

16

When the RCMP's health services called my psychiatrist's diagnosis into question, he challenged them to bring in another doctor. They didn't. After more than two years on leave, both my physician and my psychiatrist felt I'd never be well enough for active duty. They signed off on the paperwork supporting a medical discharge from the RCMP. There was no going back.

It was devastating. What was wrong with me? I had loved policing so much. I vacillated between being angry with myself and furious with the management I felt had so desperately let me down. I alternated between despondency over the loss of my career—a loss that coincided with the end of my marriage—and relief that I never had to return to a poisonous workplace and a job that made me so sick. Stirred into that confusing mix of emotions was an overriding feeling that I had failed.

Strange as it might sound, the Bumble Beary Pie Daycare turned out to be the antidote for all my despair. In our new house, the girls thrived, and so did my daycare, which we named for our love of bees and bears and to memorialize Kay's wonderful pies.

The kids and I did crafts. We sang and danced and played outside. The older ones practiced their letters, numbers, and printing. The younger ones just filled the space with their wonder. That busy hive of activity was hard work, and I went to bed exhausted every night, but I got up every morning looking forward to doing it again.

I loved those kids and their creative energy. They were a microcosm, a representation in miniature of the society I'd worked with as a police officer. There were leaders and followers, those who never spoke out and others who never kept quiet. Some were way too confident and rushed right in. Some were afraid to get their hands dirty. And some had more than their share of worries.

For Ashley and Erin, it was like having a whole bunch of little siblings to play with, to teach about nail polish and other worldly things. They saw how much work a small person really is, and I liked to think it was a great lesson in birth control and family planning for my daughters.

For me, it was a chance to reconnect to the complicated structure of community. I got to know the parents and caregivers during conversations as they picked up their kids. My parents were single moms and single dads, married couples, grandparents who were raising grandchildren, and members of extended families who'd taken charge of a child rather than see him go into foster care. In each of them, I saw myself when my kids were young, trying to balance work and family and find time for myself and my intimate relationship, too. It's so easy to get rundown and burnt out and lose your way. That much I knew, so I tried to support all those busy families who trusted me with their children.

I guess at that, I succeeded. With few exceptions, every child who came to my daycare stayed until I closed my doors.

BUT THERE WAS STILL A lot of crap to get through.

In February 2010, two weeks before my retirement from the RCMP was official—a retirement that offered a very much reduced pension, of course—a chief superintendent and the officer in charge of professional standards arrived at my house to deliver the final report of the investigation into my allegations of harassment. We sat at my dining-room table. The officer in charge of professional standards complimented my house and commented on my fish tank—pleasantries I had no interest in. Let's get this over with, I thought. I've waited long enough.

The chief superintendent drew the final report from its envelope, and they went through it paragraph by paragraph. The document began by clearly defining the RCMP policy on harassment. After a lengthy dissertation on what is and what isn't, it concludes:

> Comments or actions that would constitute harassment would normally fall in the range of serious or repeated rude, degrading or offensive remarks. In order to meet the definition of harassment, it must be established that the respondent "knew or ought reasonably to have known [the remarks] would cause offense or harm."

Below this, bold headers announced, "Allegation(s) against." The first allegation concerned the member who'd told Wayne, when we first started dating, that he'd had sex with me. Wayne recalled the conversation had taken place in a change room with no one else present. The accused denied it. "In the absence of any independent witnesses or corroborating evidence, I find the allegation unsubstantiated."

I had no idea, so early on, that by the end of these gruelling few hours I would come to hate the words "allegation unsubstantiated" so much.

Wayne also recalled being told I was the right "blow job height," but the member couldn't recall uttering it. Interestingly, the report notes that Wayne, "as a custodian...felt it would have been inappropriate for him to respond to comments made by a regular member. Wayne Merlo stated there was a hierarchy and he felt it better to put up with the environment rather than say anything."

No one could remember having seen a blow-up doll in a watch commander's office, though it had been legend around the detachment. No one remembered a request to attend aerobics being denied. No one could recall a single condescending remark about my being pregnant. Over and over: no independent witnesses, no corroborating evidence. "Unsubstantiated."

It amazed me that all of these trained police officers—investigators with years of experience in recalling facts and details—had such poor memories.

When the harassment was happening, I didn't take notes on it. I was too appalled, too embarrassed, and probably too afraid to write those things down. In hindsight, that's exactly what I should have done. Those old notations could have corroborated some of my claims. But without witnesses, without evidence, well, there isn't much an investigator can do. I understand that. What galls me are the inconsistencies in the report.

That staffing interview I was forced to take part in—the one I was later told was "an attempt to make me quit"—is an interesting case. The officer in charge remembered it but claimed it wasn't punitive. The sergeant recalled it too, even recalled my wondering why I'd never received a written report, but he denied that any negative comments ever passed between us about it. Strangely, the member who'd come to interview me couldn't dredge up any recollection of meeting with me at all. There was nothing in his notes, no paperwork, no trace that the interview had taken place. So three of us say it happened, but there's no paper trail whatsoever. That doesn't strike me as unsubstantiated. It strikes me as odd.

Similarly, the member who'd apologized for the conversation in which he and a superior carried on about "fat-assed ugly females" in the detachment remembered the incident and the apology, too. The higher ranking member did not. Since it was the superior I'd confronted about what I'd overheard, he must have told the junior member I was offended. This allegation was not unsubstantiated—rather, it was deemed to have been appropriately resolved.

Making the junior member apologize. I guess that's a resolution, RCMP style.

As for all the incidents involving the sergeant who regularly inundated me with sexually aggressive suggestions, everyone seemed to forget everything. Nobody remembered dildos or requests to kiss it better or a multitude of other vulgar incidents. Nobody substantiated any of my claims.

I wanted to know: had the investigators even spoken to the people I'd suggested? I had no way of knowing. Later, when I applied under freedom of information legislation to see the statements that were taken, I was denied access even to a list of people who had been interviewed. But during the prolonged period between making my statement and receiving the report, I did talk with women at the detachment. Many told me, when interviewed, they took advantage of the opportunity. They may not have witnessed the events I alleged, but they told investigators they weren't surprised because they'd been through similar things. None of this is reflected in the final report.

I don't blame the witnesses who said they didn't remember. They work in an organization that demands loyalty above all else. They have careers to think about—promotions they may be after, courses they may want to take, transfers they may or may not want. They have to go to work every day and trust that their co-workers have their backs. They can't very well offer a statement in support of a rat.

Near the close of their visit to my house, the chief superintendent and the Officer in charge of professional standards admitted people were afraid to speak to them. I recorded our conversation. I have them on tape acknowledging the problems in doing such an investigation and even asking me how they might overcome this reluctance.

They knew I was upset, outraged, and had lost faith in the RCMP, but they assured me they were both working to address the problem. My faith would be rebuilt, they told me, as I watched the transformation their work would create. In the nearly three years since those two sat at my dining-room table and vowed to make changes, I've not spoken to either of them again. And to this day, I've never seen them openly confront any issues of harassment.

After they left my house, I was left with the words "unsubstantiated allegations" ringing in my ears, and an official report lying useless on my dining-room table. I read through the concluding paragraphs. "Due to the extensive lapse in time between the incidents and the time you reported them, it has been difficult to corroborate…." And in the paragraph beneath that, oddly, there's an apology of sorts: "I understand that you may be disappointed in the results of the investigation. I offer my apologies to you on behalf of the RCMP for the treatment you feel you received at Nanaimo Detachment. I would also like to advise you that the RCMP is striving to eliminate harassment in the workplace…."

I flipped the report back to its beginning. It was printed on the official letterhead of the Royal Canadian Mounted Police. At the top, the world famous symbol bearing the slogan "Maintiens le droit." Underneath that appears the line "Guided By Integrity, Honesty, Professionalism, Compassion, Respect & Accountability."

After I received that final report, I gave up. I possessed neither the emotional strength nor the money to continue the fight. I had to concentrate on my girls, on running my daycare, and on recovering my sense of dignity. And I had to file for divorce.

I'd given up on that front, too. I had hoped, after the girls and I moved away, that Wayne would do some soul searching, get help, and come back to us. And he did go for help, but he gave up on it very quickly, so nothing really changed. He resigned himself to the way things were. That was a hard pill for me to swallow, but I had to move forward.

I loved Jeannie like a sister, and I knew divorcing Wayne also meant losing her. She'd never really recovered from the loss of her husband, Don. Grief clung to her. She was unable to accept that I couldn't just work things out with Wayne—she would have done anything for the chance to grow old with her husband. I understood, but I also knew her perspective was skewed, that she hadn't lived in the kind of marriage I was leaving.

For everyone's sake, I was determined to make this part, the actual legal dissolution of our bond, the most amicable divorce ever. And it was headed that way. We had no argument on the division of property and how to handle custody, so I bought a do-it-yourself divorce kit to save us money. When I proposed a settlement, Wayne initially agreed to it. But then he dug in his heels and refused to sign anything. Instead, he hired a lawyer. I didn't understand the sudden shift. I thought I'd been very fair in what I'd proposed, and I was willing to negotiate. I wasn't going after him for anything; I believed in my heart he would never abandon the girls. Finally, Wayne divulged what triggered his sudden need for legal advice: he'd found out about my payout from the RCMP, and he wanted it included in my assets.

What payout? There was no payout. I'd never asked for a dime from them, and I'd certainly never received one. He knew that.

Or he'd known that, anyway, until a conversation about separating assets in the cellblock led some RCMP member to ask how much of my payout Wayne was entitled to. Wayne's confusion was quickly allayed by the member, who assured my husband that, yes, I'd received a substantial amount of money to shut up and go away.

It was a hell of a nasty prank if that's what it was intended to be.

Wayne said at first he was sure they were wrong, there was no money, but then he'd been called into a closed-door meeting at the police station. He wouldn't tell me who called the meeting; he was afraid he'd lose his job. He claimed he was informed that I'd been given a large sum—in excess of a million dollars—and if it wasn't accounted for in my financial disclosure, I was obviously hiding it until after the divorce. Wayne made it sound like the meeting was meant as a favour to him, a way to make sure he got his fair share.

No matter how many times I insisted there'd been no payout, no matter how many times I pointed out that unsubstantiated allegations didn't warrant a whack of cash, the seed had been planted in Wayne's head and had taken root. I didn't know if Wayne had invented that meeting or if it was a clever plot by someone at the detachment to hurt me, but I had to hire a lawyer, too.

I also wrote a letter, copying it to everyone who might have convened such a meeting: the watch commander during Wayne's shift, the officer in charge of the detachment, and the municipal manager. I asked if there'd been a meeting with my estranged husband to discuss our financial settlement and, if there had been, why? I suggested that even calling such a meeting was a breach of confidentiality, was malicious, and as far as I could tell, was an admission of guilt that harassment had taken place. After all, if people in the RCMP were talking payout, they must believe I deserved it.

As usual, nobody acknowledged my letter, which only convinced me that Wayne was telling the truth. If he'd fabricated the whole thing and implicated them in wrongdoing, they would have denied it—and they would have been on him fast. At the very least, he would have been disciplined. Instead, nothing was said.

Months passed. We spent thousands of dollars on lawyers trying to resolve the impasse. I even had the lawyer in Calgary who'd been involved in my complaint confirm, in writing, that no payout had been made, but that wasn't enough for Wayne and his lawyer. They wanted word from the RCMP—and the RCMP was mute.

In the fall of 2011, I sat stunned in front of the television as CBC TV's Natalie Clancy interviewed my former troop mate, Catherine Galliford. I hadn't seen Catherine in almost twenty years, not since we'd trained together. Onscreen, she looked slender, stressed, and broken—a far cry from the vibrant, cheerful girl I remembered at Depot.

During her career, Catherine had served as the RCMP's spokesperson in two large investigations—one of them the Pickton mass-murder case. But as she explained in that interview, instead of being treated with respect, she'd faced corrosive sexual discrimination and harassment on the job. Listening to Catherine brought me to tears. So much of her story echoed my own.

I immediately sent Natalie Clancy an email in support of Catherine. In my message, I detailed a bit about my own negative experiences in the RCMP. Natalie requested an interview, but I wasn't ready to talk, and I certainly didn't feel strong and confident enough to appear on television.

I wasn't the only one who saw that interview and responded. Within days of the broadcast, over 150 female members of the RCMP contacted the CBC in support of their brave colleague. Every one of them had a story to tell—and the stories were all so similar. Suddenly, we had some insight into the scope of this problem right across the country. It was clear harassment in the RCMP wasn't just a few isolated cases. It was epidemic.

The aftermath of Catherine's disclosure pulsed out in all directions like the shock wave from a brilliant explosion. It rattled the senior ranks in the RCMP, jarred the Canadian public's perception of its national police force, and infused hundreds of female members with the courage to speak out.

In my life, its effects were immediate and far-reaching.

In the wake of Catherine's revelations on national television, members at the detachment started saying things to Wayne like, "If Janet didn't get paid out before, she sure as hell will now." He grew even more convinced that I was hiding some pot of shiny shut-up gold. He knew full well, he told me, that the RCMP wouldn't send two "bigwigs" to my house just to tell me to fuck off.

In a desperate attempt to put an end to the nonsense, I sent both of those bigwigs—the chief superintendent and the officer in charge of professional standards—an email asking them to refute the rumours of my newfound wealth. I got no reply, so I contacted Lois Karr, then the advisor to the Human resources officer for the Pacific region. She said she'd look into it on my behalf. Soon after, she called to tell me she'd spoken with the detachment, but nobody there knew what she was talking about—despite the letters I'd sent to so many of the managers. And that was that. She said she'd done all she could.

When I sat down to write yet another thousand-dollar cheque to the divorce lawyer, frustration overtook me. Between the shaking and the tears, I could barely sign my name. This ridiculous rumour was deleting our family's personal funds. Money was so tight I had nothing to spend on the girls for Christmas. Every month for almost a year, a thousand dollars had left my account and gone to the lawyer. And that was just on my side. Who knew how much Wayne was spending to try and track down my phantom million dollars.

The more I thought about it, the angrier I got. I emailed Lois Karr and told her I'd be happy to send a copy of my next legal bill to the RCMP. I also told her I'd be more than happy to contact the media if this issue wasn't resolved very soon.

I wasn't sure yet if I had the guts to follow through on that threat, but I was bolstered by Catherine's ongoing courage. After she had spoken out, the RCMP did their best to discredit Catherine through attacks on her personal character. But every attempt to destroy her credibility or shred her reputation only seemed to create another chance for Catherine to display grace under fire. She stood by her allegations; she refused to be dissuaded from telling her truth.

ASHLEY HAD RECENTLY OBTAINED HER driver's license. Over and over again, I heard myself warn her never to stop on the highway at night if a police car tried to pull her over.

You have to understand, there had been talk, in the detachment where I served, of members who engaged in inappropriate contact with young girls, stories of police officers whose sexual misconduct had been swept under the rug. I'd personally witnessed a group of male members gathered around the closed-circuit camera in the Nanaimo cellblock, leering at young women, commenting on their "nice tits." Sometimes, those attractive young women had been arrested for the slightest evidence of intoxication so they could be held overnight without charges—no lawyer, no record, no rights. Just the humiliating opportunity to be eye candy for a handful of men who thought the uniform entitled them to exploit women.

I didn't want my daughter in the locked backseat of a police car getting searched by one of those guys with no witnesses around. So I told Ashley—told her many times—that she wasn't to pull over, not out there alone. That she should drive the speed limit all the way into town, to a public lot like a gas station or a coffee shop, before she pulled over, even though that would be considered engaging in a chase.

Despite all the good officers I knew, I'd lost faith in the guarantee of protection while in the custody of the police. And if a former officer of the law was willing to counsel her daughter to break the law—if that mother was fully prepared to go to court someday and tell a judge why she'd advised her daughter not to pull over, not to take the chance of being vulnerable to a corrupt cop on a dark highway—then what might happen in society if everyone's faith in the police was busted right across this country? Anarchy. That's what the managers at the RCMP feared—the complete collapse of their authority.

Denial of wrongdoing was the only way to ensure the faith and to keep order. The more outrageous or unpleasant a complaint against an officer, the more important it was to push it out of the public eye. When allegations emerged, the crucial strategy was deny, deny, and deny. Complaints investigated internally were dismissed. The world's most famous national police force, the ones who always got their man, couldn't ever seem to find any evidence of transgression among their own.

I had finally come to fully understand why an acknowledgement of misconduct was too risky for the RCMP. Any confirmation that some members might engage in loathsome behaviour—

whether illegal or immoral—could cause rebellion against an authority that has been allowed to rule unchecked for too long. Something of a revolution might even occur, one that could knock over the powerful ladder of privilege they were all standing on.

Maintain the right. That's what it was all about—even when the right was so very wrong.

I rolled all of it over and over in my head—the harassment and gender discrimination I'd experienced, my failed attempts to find fairness, the ongoing turmoil in my family caused by the RCMP's refusal to simply provide an answer. I thought of Catherine's brave stand, about my advice to Ashley to break the law, and then I knew I could no longer justify my silence.

I sent an email to Gary Mason, a British Columbia-based writer at *The Globe and Mail* whose previous work I had admired and whom I'd been in touch with before. I told him I was ready to take off the gag and speak out about what life was like for me and for so many women in the RCMP. He got right back to me. For almost three hours, I recounted my story. I broke down crying several times, but I made it through the interview.

On December 3, 2011, *The Globe and Mail* ran a lengthy article about me and my allegations of harassment in the Saturday edition. The article detailed a handful of incidents—the dildos left in my work area, the nasty response from a superior to my first pregnancy, the refusal of higher ups to respond appropriately to inappropriate behaviour. But that day, I didn't know what the article actually said because I never picked up a copy of the paper. I never left the house. I stayed in my pajamas, terrified about the fallout and puking all day long.

The most immediate reaction came from online news commenters. Their stream of vitriol was constant and caustic. I tried to focus on all the reasons I had gone to the media, to think about all the times I'd wanted to speak out but hadn't. Still, it was hard to counter my sense of regret at having thrust myself into the spotlight.

I only got through those first hard weeks by relying on the collective strength of another online community—one I'd helped to create. After Catherine came out publicly, I got in touch with a couple of the women who'd also spoken up. That's when I realized we needed our own Facebook group. I had previously created one for the families at my daycare and found it a simple way to exchange information. We dubbed it Girls Together for Better and made the group invitation-only. It quickly became a place to share our stories, to just say whether or not we were having a good day or a falling-apart day. It was a safe haven, and as much as anything can be, the page was private.

Many of us were weak and vulnerable. Sometimes a person had to step away when a comment triggered a bad reaction, so we carefully screened everyone who wanted to join. At first it was only women, but eventually it became a safe place for some of the males who'd suffered from bullying—who knew all about being called "pussies" and having to keep their mouths shut, who also suffered from anxiety attacks, sleep troubles, depression, financial worries, and all the other hard things our careers had imposed on our lives. We all wanted the same thing—we wanted to unite, to lean on each other until we were stronger, to create change that one day would help make the RCMP healthier, as well.

I'd long believed the RCMP would offer a better workplace if its members were unionized, so this small example of collective voice gave me great satisfaction.

MAKING GOOD ON MY THREAT to go to the media seemed to be productive. Just a few days after *The Globe and Mail* ran my story, a letter was sent from the human resources officer in Vancouver to Wayne's lawyer, confirming there hadn't been any financial settlement and that there were no ongoing negotiations. After nearly a year of my begging them to dispel the bullshit so we could settle our divorce, it was done. I'm certain my willingness to go to the media convinced them to write that letter.

After he received it, Wayne called me crying, sorry that he'd believed their lies. We were out thousands of dollars each for legal fees. I told him I wished, after so many years of marriage, that he could have trusted me over them. But he was adamant—he said they had been so convincing.

The divorce went through easily after that. Mostly I was relieved, but one afternoon when I was walking the waterfront and the bells at the Anglican church began to peel, I broke into tears and had to sit down on a bench. "That's our church," I whispered.

Changing Worlds

17

After the lawyer called to say the divorce was final, I drove to Long Beach, outside Tofino, and walked my beloved beach an unmarried woman. The waves kept pouring in and everything seemed such a bittersweet relief.

In April 2012, I walked that beach again after two more big changes had come in my life. On March 27, I had filed a civil class-action lawsuit in the Supreme Court in British Columbia against the RCMP, alleging sexual harassment. Strangely, it was the Facebook group that sparked the class-action suit by lending combined strength and spurring us into collective action. Natalie Clancy at CBC, who covered the story of the lawsuit's launch, told me that as far as she knew, it was the first time social media had been used to reach out to victims of a crime and unite them in a lawsuit against the government.

One among us had contacted the lawyers, and then others did, and they asked the group for as much information as we could provide. All the letters and statements I'd written and all the responses I'd received—or not received—were suddenly very valuable. I was chosen as the representative plaintiff not because I'd suffered more than others, but because I had a substantial paper trail, including a statement already vetted through a lawyer.

When asked to put my name on the lawsuit, I said yes without hesitation. I had nothing left to lose. Besides, for years I'd been begging for somebody to listen. Here was my chance. I should have been standing tall—there were over one hundred and fifty women standing behind me, sharing their stories so the immense scope of the problem could emerge. Even public support was more apparent every day. I knew it was all necessary and important, but on March 27, I'd spent the day vomiting and hyperventilating, scared to death about being the one named, the one so visibly standing up against the bully.

Another massive decision heralded a big change in my life. I'd decided to leave British Columbia after twenty years and go home. The house had been sold, the closing was in May, and the girls and I were leaving behind the years of turmoil to re-establish ourselves on the other side of the country. I looked forward to that new beginning, but I was mourning, too. On that last Long Beach walk, I wept, knowing I might never come back again. This place was so sacred to me that when Wayne and I, years earlier, had made our funeral arrangements, my wishes were to be cremated and have my ashes spread here on this thundering Pacific beach.

With a piece of driftwood, I wrote, "Goodbye Tofino" in the sand, and I vowed to return someday a strong, confident woman.

There were so many more goodbyes out in front of me. The day Bumble Beary Pie Daycare closed forever, I could hardly hold back my tears. Saying goodbye to the Stitch & Bitch group was also tough. On my final night, they presented me with a mug that had a cross-stitched liner. They'd each stitched a meaningful part of it. It's among my most cherished possessions, along with my memories of those Wednesday nights.

And Winona—just finishing her radiation treatments—leaving her was agonizing. She presented me with a t-shirt with all the names of our Friday night pub crew, and she promised to come visit Newfoundland when she was strong enough to travel. I told her we'd take a road trip on my eastern island when she came, have a high time eating fish 'n chips and visiting little shops in outport communities.

But there were so many reasons to leave Vancouver Island, so many potential enemies lurking around every corner. I still feared that Wayne might snap and make good on his threats to kill me rather than let me go. Getting out of Nanaimo was a first step in escaping so much of the past, and I didn't really feel safe until the girls and I were through security at the airport and boarding the plane.

IF I'D NEVER JOINED THE RCMP, I'd have missed out on so much fulfilment in my life. In addition to meeting my husband, having my beautiful daughters, and enjoying some truly great years with wonderful friends in British Columbia, my career allowed me to make a valuable contribution and to interact across a broad spectrum of society. I take away from my policing career so much knowledge and experience, a more complete understanding of human nature than I can imagine having found anywhere else. I was honoured to work alongside some truly dedicated and amazing police officers. I am proud to now be taking part in a difficult process that I hope will strengthen the RCMP, improving the organization for future members.

But while I try to remain positive, I am sometimes overwhelmed by my anger at the RCMP for failing, so dramatically, those it should have protected and honoured.

I've seen so many comments suggesting that the women who signed on to the class-action suit—over two hundred by 2013—were in it for the money. I've been called a gold-digger, and worse.

No amount of money can bring back what we sacrificed to serve in the RCMP. We have all lost so much in varying degrees. We lost our marriages, our pensions, our health, the security we wanted for our children, our self-respect, and confidence. We lost our reason to get up and get out there, to feel proud of the tough career we'd chosen. But we didn't come together to ask for money. That's not what this is about. I've spent thousands of dollars of my own already and never asked for five cents. We have demanded change.

There have been glimmers of change—though whether or not it's posturing for the media I can't say. I've read news stories claiming the RCMP has overhauled its discipline and transfer practices so members can't escape accountability for wrongdoing. And I hope the impetus to change the organization is genuine because there are more good guys than bad on the force, and they deserve to regain the public's trust, to serve in an organization that exhibits the same integrity and commitment to service that the majority of its individual members do.

In 2011, after Catherine Galliford came forward and a wave of women followed, the RCMP continued to deny all the allegations. Two years later, they committed to training two hundred officers to investigate harassment complaints. An issue that didn't exist twenty-four months prior had grown into what the RCMP Commissioner called a "sexual harassment crisis."

Change is a slow process, and class-action suits move at a glacial pace. I'm told this will take years to wind its way through the courts. In the meantime, I'm working hard to put my life back together.

The girls and I live in a small house in a nice neighbourhood of St. John's. Soon after we moved, Ashley found a job at a restaurant. Erin, too, has started to work, and during her first winter here, she fell in love with skiing. At such a young age, a time when leaving friends behind is so hard, they have both handled the move across the country with grace and style, and have settled into new friendships and new routines. My relationship with my daughters continues to be close and strong; they are my rock and my compass.

Both girls are in touch with their father and are working on strengthening that relationship. As for Wayne, he continues to work in the Nanaimo prison cellblock and suffers the brunt of hostility that my allegations have attached to his last name. I am sorry about that, and I wish for him peace.

Now based on the other side of the country from where I wore the uniform, I find myself employed on the opposite side of corrections. I work with the John Howard Society, an organization committed to the belief that justice is best served through measures that resolve conflicts, repair harm, and restore harmony. Like mine, their core values include the intrinsic worth of every person, the right to be treated with dignity, equity, fairness, and compassion. They stress that the right to live in a safe, peaceful society must be balanced by the responsibility to respect the law.

In the short time I've worked with the John Howard Society, I've found it tremendously rewarding to be part of something that helps people get their lives back on track—something I had once hoped to do through a career in policing. One night soon after I started at Howard House, a supervised transitional home for ex-offenders, a former resident called from Alberta to let us know our programs had helped him completely turn his life around. He was working full time and was a thriving member of society. And he was grateful. That's a process I hope to contribute to in some small way. I am also grateful that I'm getting my life back on track, too. While I never committed any crime, I did get mired in problems and lose my way; I lost myself and so much of what I valued.

My new job has me working alone at night quite often, and that's important for me as I heal. I find solitude stops my mind from racing, from careering into a frenzy.

I continue to suffer from the years of stress I experienced, and I'm prone to crying jags when I talk about the past. Oddly, it's worse when talking about the good times, remembering my early days in the RCMP when I was so committed to my work, the happy years Wayne and I spent together, and the dear friends in Nanaimo I've had to leave behind.

I still suffer, too, from the effects of post traumatic stress disorder. Many people with PTSD never fully escape the memories and images that haunt them. Some turn to drugs and alcohol, falling victim to the evils they used to avoid the disorder. Certain things can trigger a landslide in my brain. I still get very anxious in crowds. I've developed an aversion to smells, such strong triggers to memories, so I can't even walk through a department store past the fragrance counters. I also find it distressing in a public place like a restaurant if there's someone who's talking too loudly, or looking around as if they need to make sure they've caught the attention of everyone else. I can't quite explain why, but it tenses me up and makes me want to scream.

Still, there are far fewer triggers here in Newfoundland. I never have to cruise past the site of some gruesome scene I attended. There is no cracked concrete here that can send me into a tailspin or spark a series of nightmares. And while my house doesn't have a fireplace, if I can't sleep, I can gaze out the window from my bed and see the city lights and Signal Hill in the distance. On a clear day, I can see the ocean and find comfort in knowing I am safe in this home.

THE ROOTS OF ALL I am, every turn my life has taken, go back to my childhood. I believe my experiences at school instilled in me a reluctance to challenge authority, and that merged with my innate need to succeed and, more importantly, to please others, leading me to accept things at home and at work that few others would put up with. But I can also see how my parents' love, respect, and guidance gave me the core strength to hold on to what I value and to recover myself, to heal.

It was so important for me to come home, to live closer to Mom and Dad. Just as I'd been there in the final years to help care for Jack and Kay Merlo, I wanted to be there for my parents, to share those years. And I wanted Erin and Ashley to really know and appreciate this other set of adoring grandparents.

THE SUMMER I RETURNED TO Newfoundland after such a long absence, my parents were approaching their fiftieth wedding anniversary. To celebrate, what they wanted most was for all their children and grandchildren to come together, so they planned a family retreat at Kilmory Resort on the Burin Peninsula. Kilmory sits on a wide estuary where the Piper's Hole River mixes with the saltwater of Placentia Bay. Each A-frame cabin has a spectacular view of the water and the hills beyond. The whole setting is wonderfully tranquil, but as I drove into the resort, I felt anything but tranquil.

Our family has been lucky—we've avoided disease, violence, addiction, and other tragedies, but we've had our share of problems, most of them associated with distance. We lived so far apart for so long, scattered in different parts of the country, that we lost the grace of easy interaction and never had special family gatherings. Through the years, our connections to each other grew thin. This golden anniversary would be the first time in twenty years that my brothers and I were in the same place, and the first time Erin and Ashley would meet their cousins.

I'd missed my brothers, but I was nervous about seeing them. They were both successful in their careers and their marriages, and here I was divorced and making a public spectacle of myself in the media. I desperately wanted us to knit together as a family again.

Ashley and Erin had absorbed some of my trepidation on the two-hour drive from St. John's, so they were jumpy, too, as we clambered out beside the cabin the three of us would share with my parents. I knew my brothers and their families were nearby. What I didn't know was how they might judge me now or whether they felt I had failed to live up to expectations. There was a knot in my stomach. I didn't know if I could manage two days of it.

As it turned out, the only problem with our Kilmory weekend was that it wasn't long enough. There was a brief period of awkwardness, and then Dad said, "Come on, we gotta get a picture of all of you together." For the first time in over two decades, I stood beside my brothers, smiling for the camera. Our stiffness dissolved. We were a family again.

And then it was just fun, all the catching up conversations and the outside games, the barbeques and swimming. Every time I looked at my parents, they were beaming.

On the last afternoon, I rented a kayak and headed out into the estuary for a few hours alone. I paddled for a while, and then I turned and looked back toward the resort. I could make out the noise coming from the swimming pool—Erin and Ashley laughing with their cousins like they were all old friends. I could hear my brothers' voices, relaxed and strong. And on the shore, at the water's edge, my father stood looking out at me.

In that moment—at least for that moment—I knew that I had not let anyone down, that I had simply done the best I could through the years. For a change then, the tears that gathered were not from grief or shame but from relief. There was no point sitting out alone in a kayak and thinking about what could have been. Joy had found a way to edge in, and here was a chance to open a new notebook and fill it with better memories.

The water was serene, barely rippling with the tide, when I turned and paddled to shore.

JANET MERLO WITH HER DAUGHTERS, ERIN AND ASHLEY.

JANET MERLO is a retired member of the RCMP. Originally from Harbour Grace, Merlo now lives with her two daughters in St. John's, Newfoundland. She is the representative plaintiff in a proposed class-action lawsuit against the RCMP.